HEADLIGHT PRESS Presents:

Gospel Seeds

The Poetry of John David Harrell

Published by
HEADLIGHT PRESS
6500 Clito Road, Statesboro, Georgia 30461

ISBN 10: 1-58535-274-8
ISBN 13: 978-1-58535-274-6

John David Harrell was born on January 9, 1943. He was born in McRae, Georgia, with Dr. Frank Mann, Sr. attending. Dr. Mann told John David's parents, John Willie and Marjorie Harrell, that he would not live more than a few days at the most due to convulsions he suffered at birth. John David will celebrate his 73rd birthday in 2016.

John David attended first grade through fourth grade at Towns Elementary School and then transferred to McRae-Elementary School in McRae, Georgia, where he finished the eighth grade. He attended Telfair County High and graduated in 1961, after having perfect attendance for 12 straight years. John David attended South Georgia Vocational and Technical School, Americus, Georgia, from 1961-1963, and received a certificate in Cabinet and Woodworking. Then John David returned home where he worked in the family business - farming and egg production. For 17 years John David worked in the family business while attending the Presbyterian Church in McRae.

After working on the farm, John David went to work for the City of Jacksonville, Georgia, in the Sanitation and Water Works Department. He was also a Volunteer Firefighter for the city. John David was involved in community affairs as a Boy Scout Leader and a Lions Club member. He joined Blockhouse Baptist Church in Jacksonville, Georgia, in 1973, and has taught Sunday School and Bible School there for the last 40 years. John David also volunteered as a Bible teacher at the state prison in McRae, Georgia, working with male inmates.

John David began writing poetry in 1992, and found this was a great passion for his life, as well as a gift from the Lord. He has written almost 100 poems, some of which expound on scriptures from the Bible. He has also written poems depicting family life growing up on the farm.

Although John David has had many physical challenges, he has used his talents wisely and has tried to bless others with his gifts. He would like to share his poetry with others to lead them to Christ, to bless God's children, and to declare his love for the Lord.

John David would like to thank Brother Robert Wigley who has been a faithful friend and mentor to him during the last forty or fifty years. Readers can also find John David's poetry in some of Brother Wigley's books on Daniel and Revelation. Also, he would like to thank Brother Wigley's wife, Janice, for proofreading his poetry and offering suggestions. Additionally, John David would like to thank the Lions Club of Jacksonville, Georgia, for their help to him in obtaining a hearing aid and for their encouragement.

John David would like to dedicate this book to his mother and father, John Willie Harrell and Marjorie Nell Harrell who brought him up in the admonition of the Lord, teaching him that "nothing is impossible with God", and teaching him Christian values and the value of hard work. Also, he would like to thank all of his teachers throughout the years for their patience in giving him instruction as he had many obstacles to learning.

1

THE MOUNTAINS

The mountains in my life are steep and very hard to climb,
Yet as I reach for the top, there the face of God I find.
The mountains in my life are rough, as along the trail I stumble,
Yet with each barrier that I cross, my life grows more humble.

The mountains in my life challenge to develop body and mind,
Yet with each challenge, I learn true strength in God I find.
The mountains in my life bring thirst as I walk along the trail,
Yet from the springs, my soul is refreshed from His deepest well.

The mountains in my life bring fear as I face the dangers there,
Yet as I follow in His footsteps, my life I place in His care.
The mountains in my life bring joy, when to the top I reach,
And there I sit with my Lord, His truths to me He doth teach.

The mountains in my life bring peace, when God's word I share,
And I look into the hearts of others and see the beauty there.
The mountains in my life bring understanding as I go uphill,
That I may have more compassion when I learn to do God's Will.

You see, I must climb the mountain to meet our God from above,
That I might show to others, the nature of His wonderful love.

February 1993

Genesis 22:2; Exodus 3:1; Exodus 3:12; Psalms 11:1; Psalms 30:7;
Isaiah 2:2-3; Isaiah 11:9; Isaiah 30:25; Isaiah 30:29; Isaiah 40:9;
Joel 2:1; Zephaniah 3:11; Matthew 14:23; Luke 3:5; Revelation 21:1

Mountains are mentioned 144 times in God's word. Abraham, Moses and Jesus had special experiences on mountains. In Genesis 22:14 Abraham called the name of the Mount Jehovah-jireh: meaning the Lord will provide (Genesis 22:8). Moses also met God on a mountain where he saw the burning bush. Jesus faced His greatest trials on mountains when Satan tempted Him and He overcame temptation by the Word of God (Matthew 4). Jesus went to the mountains often to pray to His Father (Matthew 14:23). When the Bible speaks of mountains it can mean peace or times of trial. When Joe Ward and I hiked the north Georgia Appalachian Trail, I was surprised to find so many springs close to the tops of the mountains. It was good, clear and cold. Sometimes it could get too cold when you needed a bath after several days on the trail. After hiking for ten days on the trail, Joe Ward and I were on our way to Amicalola Falls to get his truck. On the way to the check-out station we met some girls who wanted to know where we had hiked. After we told them about our trip, we started on down the trail. Joe was ahead of me so he did not hear what I heard. One of the girls said, *"They smell like they've been up there ten days!"*

The Bible says we are to be a peculiar people (Deut. 14:2). This was referring to the nation of Israel. I Peter 2:9 also mentions this in reference to the Church. The girls thought we were peculiar but in a different way. God thinks of Israel and the Church as His special treasure (Ps. 135:4). We are set aside to serve Him.

2

SUNSET

Sunset on the mountain is a beautiful sight to see.
Sunset on the mountain is there for you and me.

Sunset on the mountain brings peace to a weary heart.
Sunset on the mountain brings rest for a new day's start.

When we travel on the mountain, our bodies grow tired and weak.
But at the end of the day, the sunset comes as we reach the peak.

I have seen many sunsets but the most beautiful has been,
On top of some rugged mountain where the world seems to end.

Jesus meets us on the mountain where He died on Calvary.
He gave His life on the mountain; from sin, He sets us free.

January 1998

Exodus 17:12; Exodus 22:26; Deut. 23:11; Mark 1:32; Matthew 14:23;
Mark 3:13; Luke 6:12; Matthew 11:28-29; Mark 14:41;
John 19:17; Luke 23:33

Sunsets are truly beautiful at the end of a blessed and beneficial day. Some of the most beautiful sunsets I've seen have been in the mountains of north Georgia. I've also seen many beautiful sunsets in Telfair County, Georgia, where I grew up on the farm. In the days when horses and mules were used to do farm work, a tenant farmer had started plowing his field at daybreak. He had taken a short break at noon and eaten his meager meal of biscuits, ham and syrup. He was looking forward to sunset and a good evening meal with his family, which we southerners call supper. The rows of cotton were long and that evening was even longer. The farmer grew weary and began to look up at the sun which seemed to hang in one place. The old mule sensing the farmer's feelings began to glance toward the barn. When the farmer thought he could not take another step behind the plow, he looked at the sun and put his feelings into words. "Hang there dang ye; You'll be there when I come back tomorrow."

There was another long day when our Lord Jesus was crucified on Mount Calvary. He spent many hours being betrayed, denied, tried, beaten, spat upon, carrying His cross and ours and being nailed to the cross so we might have eternal life. He remained on the cross while His life blood was drained. He was sinless, yet He took our sins and cast them into the sea as far as the east is from the west. Jesus spent many hours on the mountains around Galilee praying to His father. He saw many sunsets and sunrises as He meditated on what He would have to face. His last prayer was, "Father, forgive them, for they know not what they do."

Have you received that forgiveness?

3

THE SHEPHERD

The Shepherd calls His sheep and they hear His voice.
The Shepherd calls His sheep and they follow by choice.
The Shepherd calls His sheep to rest for the night.
The Shepherd calls His sheep and He knows them by sight.

The Shepherd knows His sheep and if they go astray,
He calls them by name and helps them find the way.
This Shepherd is the one who shows us the way.
This Shepherd is the one who teaches us to pray.

This Shepherd is the one who guides us each day.
This Shepherd is the one who helps us not to stray.
He is the good Shepherd that gives us loving care.
He is the good Shepherd who helps us to prepare.

He is the good Shepherd, the one that comes from God.
He is the good Shepherd----Our staff and our rod.
He calls to His sheep with a soft and gentle voice.
Do we seek to follow Him and make Him our choice?

Jesus is the Shepherd that comes to show the way.
Jesus is the Shepherd that teaches us how to pray.

January 1998

Ezekiel 34; Zechariah 13:7-9; Matthew 25:31-46; Matthew 26:31-32;
John 10:1-39; Hebrews 13:20-21

I know very little about sheep, but growing up on a farm in Georgia, I do know about farm animals. We had cows, hogs, horses, chickens and goats; goats being the most stubborn. When I helped daddy with a project on the farm and we finished it with satisfaction, he would say to me, *"Son, two heads are better than one, even if one is a goat-head."* I knew that daddy was just kidding with me because he loved to pick at those he loved.

Goats are hard-headed and get into a lot of trouble. At one time we had over 500 head. In the fall and winter we would keep them in the woodlands to clean up the undergrowth. Under normal circumstances they were fine with plenty to eat and drink, but with 500 head it's hard to tell if they are alright. We would have to walk through the woods to check on them ever so often. Goats are like people and often think that the grass is greener on the other side. While walking through the woods to see if everything was alright, I heard a bleating sound and went to check on it. I found a half-grown (kid) goat with his head hung in the fence. His head would go through the opening but because he had horns, he would hang in the wire when he tried to pull out. He had probably been there for a couple of days. When I got him out of the fence, he ran straight for the water hole in the branch.

As sheep of the Good Shepherd (Jesus), sometimes we act like goats and go astray looking for greener grass and get hung up with what is not good for us. Jesus leaves the 99 behind and comes to our rescue. Jesus is our living water and our bread of life. He is the one who meets all our needs.

4

THE TEACHER

Come go with me down by the sea to a place called Galilee.
Come go with me down by the sea to experience joy you see.
Come go with me down by the sea to hear His precious voice.
Come go with me down by the sea to praise Him and rejoice.

Come hear the blessed Savior when He speaks of God's love.
Come hear the blessed Savior as He shares words from above.
Come hear the blessed Savior as He teaches us to be kind.
Come hear the blessed Savior as He heals the sick and blind.

Come hear the blessed Savior as He reaches far out to you.
Come hear the blessed Savior as He proves God's word true.
Come hear the blessed Savior as He deals with man's strife.
Come hear the blessed Savior as He gives to men new life.

Come hear the blessed Savior as He touches the hearts of men.
Come hear the blessed Savior as He makes them whole again.
He is the master teacher who taught God's word at Galilee.
So that all mankind might come to know how to be set free.

February 1993

Matthew 23:7-8; John 1:38; John 1:49; John 3:2; John 3:26;
John 6:25; 1 Tim. 2:7; 2 Tim. 1:11

Next to parents, family teachers are the most important people in a child's life. They have a lot of influence on a child at a very young age. A child's knowledge and the use of that knowledge depends greatly on their teacher. My first school teacher was a fine lady and one who taught me for four years. Some might say I stayed in the same grade for four years. Mrs. Steverson actually taught the first through fourth grades at Towns School between McRae and Lumber City, Georgia, in the 1940s and 50s. It had to be tough keeping up with that many grades, lessons and assignments. Not only did she teach, but was responsible for our safety and well being. No easy task with knuckle-heads like Johnny Harrell and James Gilleon to deal with!

Then there are Sunday School teachers and Bible School teachers and Pastors who deal with our spiritual side of life. For me, these are the most important teachers we will have next to the master teacher himself, which is Jesus. They teach us the basics of how to live and treat our fellow man. We can study the word of God for years and still not understand the real meaning of living the Christian life. Without the teachings of Jesus, by the Holy Spirit, our lives change very little, but when we allow the Spirit of God to speak to us in that still small voice, our lives are changed. This allows us to have that personal relationship with Him. He can guide us through every trial in life if we allow Him to teach us His ways. We can have knowledge without wisdom, but we need truth to set us free.

5

CORNERSTONE

The stone became a stumbling block to all who did reject.
The stone became a comforter to all He did elect.

The stone became strength to make the weak strong.
The stone became a judge to break the feet of wrong.

Jesus is the cornerstone that was rejected by man.
Jesus is the cornerstone not built by human hands.

Jesus is the cornerstone on which our lives are built.
Jesus is the cornerstone that takes away our guilt.

Jesus is the cornerstone that bears all our strife.
Jesus is the cornerstone that fits into our life.

Jesus is the cornerstone that became a stumbling block.
Jesus is the cornerstone that became a solid rock.

May 1995

Job 38:6; Psalm 118:22; Isaiah 19:13; Isaiah 28:16; Zechariah 10:4;
Matthew 21:42; Mark 12:10-11; Luke 20:17; Acts 4:11; Ephesians 2:20-22;
1 Peter 2:4-8; Zechariah 4:7; Daniel 2:34; Zechariah 3:9

With the little knowledge I have of construction, I do know that without a firm foundation the building or project will collapse. You may have a very beautiful building, but without a strong foundation, you have nothing. You can also have a building that looks like it will fall at any time, but because of the foundation, it can stand for years. Many people are building their lives on worldly security that will last only for a short time when they need to build for that which will last for eternity. Ephesians 2:19-22 says that Jesus is the Chief Cornerstone of the household of God. He is the foundation upon which we build our lives. I Peter 2:5 says we are living stones built into a special house acceptable to God. We are fitted together perfectly by Jesus, the Master Carpenter, to make His temple.

When I first noticed the house in the picture below, I did not see the house behind it. I like to take photos of old buildings, so when I came back, I brought my camera. It was then that I noticed the big house in the background. What a comparison this picture made. When I see a house like this, I wonder who lived there. Was it a home filled with love for one another and God? Did they care for each member of their family? Did they share their sad times as well as their good times with each other? Did they pray to God, thanking Him for His blessings, and asking Him for guidance and help in times of trial? This is what the family of God is all about.

6

FIERY FURNACE

Into the fiery furnace the three Hebrew children went.
Into the fiery furnace, but they came out without a scent.

They would not bow nor bend; but neither would they burn.
They trusted in their God and His favor they did earn.

That furnace was heated seven times as hot as normally.
But there they stood within the flames as safe as they could be.

The King looked: he was amazed and frightened to the core.
Three were put into the fire but he saw not three but four.

The forth man had a special look, like the son of God was He.
The King just stared in amazement, who could this fourth man be?

The King cried, "Come out, come out" and three came out, you see.
The fourth man stayed in the fire: He's there for you and me.

March 1995

Daniel 3:1-30; Job 13:15; Psalm 28:1; Isaiah 51:12-13; Matthew 10:28; Matthew 10:32-33; Matthew 10:39; Matthew 16:2; Luke 12:3-9; Acts 4:10-13; Acts 4:19; Acts 5:29-32; Rev. 2:10-11; Rev. 12:11

When I worked for the city of Jacksonville, Georgia, I was also a voluntary fireman. Most firefighters in rural areas are volunteers. Our job was to save property and lives, but we needed training and experience to do the job. We had training classes taught by experienced firefighters. One of those classes was taught in Lumber City, Georgia, where we got to burn a condemned house. In one corner of a room in the house, a heat barrier was built so a fire could be built without burning the building down too quickly. We had to enter this room with full firefighting gear, including air tanks. We sat on the floor while the instructor talked about what we might face under these conditions. At one point, we were asked to remove our air mask. When we did, it was hard to breathe because of the heat and smoke. The instructor had a small container of diesel fuel which he sprayed on the fire and caused it to flare up. I don't know if it was seven times as hot, but it was hot enough for us. We were also taught not to open a door when it was hot. When you did the flames would leap-out and you could lose your life. The three Hebrew children were put into a furnace heated seven times hotter than normal. Some say that these men survived because they fell down in the chamber and the heat was at the top. This will work if the fire is not intense, but this will not help if the temperature is over a thousand (1,000) degrees. God's word says that the heat was so great that those that put them into the furnace were killed. Do not wait too late. Get down and get out!

7

WALK ACROSS THE MOUNTAINS

I have walked across the mountains and have seen the beauty there.
I have had a glimpse of Heaven, God's glory He did share.
As I walked across the mountains and touched the highest peak,
I place my hands in His hands and my soul He takes to keep.

When I walk across the mountains, the Spirit guides the way.
He guides each step that I take so I would not go astray.
When I walk across the mountains Jesus meets my every need,
And when my life grows weak and tired, my soul He doth feed.

I walked through the valleys where my spirit received rest.
That I might go through the desert my soul put to the test.
As I came to the valleys where my Lord took me by the hand,
I walked with Him and learned from Him about His holy plan.

I have been down in the valley and heard my Lord speak to me,
About His plan of salvation and His desire to set men free.
I have been in the lowest valley and touched the highest hill,
But the greatest moment in my life is when my soul He did fill.

He took me from the valley and took me to the highest place.
And I got a glimpse of Heaven and of His glory a little taste.
When I came into the barren desert, my soul in its weakness tried,
My voice went up to Heaven, "Where aren't thou, O Lord?" I cried.

When I came into the desert, I thought my life empty and bear.
I had no one in the desert, no friends I thought who did care.
When I reached out for someone, I heard His voice sound clear.
"I've been here all the time, my child, in your heart so near."

I have walked with you step by step through each daily thorn.
I have seen your pain and sufferings when your life was torn.
I have given you the strength to face every one of your woes.
I have stood there beside you and help fight off your foes.
January 1995

Some of the most wonderful times of my life have been spent in the north Georgia mountains on the Appalachian Trail. I know that others like the oceans or open plains and I like these as well. We can see beauty almost everywhere we go if we look for it. I also saw beauty along the banks of Sugar Creek, near Cedar Park, where I grew up, and along the Ocmulgee River near Jacksonville, Georgia, where I now live. God created all of nature for us to enjoy, but we need to take care of what He has entrusted us with. We are given three-score-and-ten (or seventy years) according to God's word, some more or less. How we spend that short time, and it is short, believe me, will determine how we spend eternity. Our spiritual walk with God is very much like our walk through the mountains of north Georgia. When we get to those beautiful spots in life we tend to forget about God and remember that He is the one who gives us the blessings of life. When we look around and see all that we have, we say to ourselves, look at the things I've accomplish-ed. In Daniel 4:30, Nebuchadnezzar spoke words to this effect and ended up in the wilderness for seven years. When that time was up he began to give God the credit and told his subjects to do the same. Some might say he should have given Daniel the credit but Daniel would have none of that. God will take us to those beautiful places in life to teach us His truth, but when we fail to listen, He allows us to come to the end of our rope, then we call on Him for help and find out He was there all along.

Exodus 20:18; Psalm 78:40; Psalm 78:52; Isaiah 43:19-20;
Isaiah 65:25; Joel 3:18; Matthew 17:1; Mark 1:3-4; Mark 1:12-13;
2 Peter 1:18; Rev. 17:3; Rev. 21:10

8

A LAMP

The word of God is like a lamp to guide and show the way.
It brightens up the path we take so we might not go astray.

The word of God is like a lamp to change the hearts of men.
It shines into their darkened lives and cleans away their sin.

The word of God is like a lamp bringing warmth to the soul.
Filling hearts with the love of God to take away the cold.

The word of God is like a lamp, shining brightly on a hill.
It transports men to Calvary where Christ's blood did spill.

The word of God is like a lamp shining brightly on the road.
It lights the path to cavalry and helps us bear the load.

September 2000

Genesis 15:17; Exodus 27:20; 1 Samuel 3:3; 2 Samuel 22:29;
1 Kings 15:4; Job 12:5; Psalm 119:105; Psalm 132:17;
Proverbs 6:23; Proverbs 13:9; Proverbs 20:20; Isaiah 62:1;
Rev. 8:10; Psalm 43:3;Proverbs 6:23; Ephesians 5:13;
2 Peter 1:19

When we were growing up on the farm, my brother Marion and I, liked to hunt. We hunted mostly squirrels and small game with shotguns. We liked to go coon hunting, but we did not have hunting dogs, but our neighbor, John, had some fine coon dogs. He would come to our house on Saturday night and we would hunt on our property till midnight. Sunday morning we had to be in church. On one of our hunts, Marion and I had flashlights and John was carrying the .22 rifle. We were dressed for the weather, which was in the 40s, and it was fairly dark, and that was good for hunting. When the dogs got on the trail of a coon, we were in the pecan orchard where a branch was located. We stopped to listen to see if the dogs would tree the coon. When we knew that the dogs had treed the coon, we decided to take a short cut through the branch. Then we got to the middle of the branch where Marion was in front of me and John was behind. At this point, there was a stream of water about three inches deep and three feet wide. In the excitement Marion and I jumped the stream but forgot that John had no light. When I heard a splash, I looked back and saw that John had fallen into the water. We got our coon, but it was a *wet* night for John. Job 12:25 says, *"They grope in darkness without light."* 2 Peter 1:19 says, *"And we have the word of the prophets made more certain, and you will do well to pay attention to it, as to a light shining in a dark place, until the day dawns and the morning star rises in your hearts."* John 9:5 says, *"As long as I am in the world, I am the light of the world."* And then Matthew 5:14, *"Ye are the light of the world. A city that is set on a hill cannot be hid."*

9

Wisdom

Jesus, teach me the wisdom I need to be true.
Jesus, teach me the wisdom I need to serve you.

Jesus, teach me the wisdom I need from the start.
Jesus, teach me the wisdom I need in my heart.

Jesus, teach me the wisdom that helps me to live.
Jesus, teach me the wisdom that helps me forgive.

Jesus, teach me the wisdom to live the best I can.
Jesus, teach me the wisdom to reach the souls of men.

Jesus, teach me the wisdom that I need to know.
Jesus, teach me the wisdom that I need to grow.

November 2000

Proverbs 2:6; Proverbs 2:10; Proverbs 2:12; Proverbs 4:5-7;
Proverbs 19:8; Eccles. 2:26; Isaiah 28:29; Matthew 12:42;
1 Cor. 3:19; James 3:13; 2 Peter 3:15

Have you ever met someone who knew it all? They have an answer for every problem and situation that comes up. When I meet someone like that, I usually take what they say with a grain of salt. Even the best computer will blow a circuit when it gets too much information. Solomon is considered the wisest man in the bible, yet he messed things up. He let his wives lead him into false religions. True wisdom comes from God (Jehovah), and Solomon had prayed for wisdom (1 Kings 4:29). God also gave him a great nation with riches. God gives us blessings but sometimes we use those in the wrong ways. Proverbs 2:6 says, *"For the Lord gives wisdom: out of His mouth comes knowledge and understand-ing."* Proverbs 2:10-12 says, *"When wisdom enters into your heart, and knowledge is pleasant unto thy soul; Discretion shall preserve you, understanding shall keep you: To deliver thee from the way of the evil man, from the man that speaks forward things; Forward can be interpreted as perverse or evil."* I Cor. 3:19 states, *"For the wisdom of this world is foolishness with God. For it is written, He takes the wise in their own craftiness."* We cannot mix worldly wisdom and Godly wisdom. This is like mixing too much water with your soup. It only weakens it so it has no strength. We can take worldly wisdom and succeed in worldly things and lose our spiritual blessing, or we can take Godly wisdom and succeed in both. We may not have as many worldly things, but we will be better off because the things of God are eternal (Luke 18:29-30).

10

My Life

I live my life for Jesus; I live for Him each day.
I live my life for Jesus and trust Him all the way.

He is my Lord and Savior; He gives me faith to win.
He is my Lord and Savior and on Him I can depend.

He sees me through each trial that comes to burden me.
He sees me through each trial and Satan he doth flee.

I love my Lord and Savior; He is my dearest friend.
I love my Lord and Savior and on Him I can depend.

When Jesus comes again and splits the eastern sky,
Will men not see and wonder and ask the reason why?

They have not accepted the King of Kings so dear,
Keeping His words in their hearts that He might be near.

May 1998

Psalm 4:5; Psalm 9:10; Psalm 13:5; Psalm 20:7; Psalm 62:8; Proverbs
3:5;
Isaiah 26:4; John 14:1; Matthew 6:30;
Matthew 9:22; Matthew 16:8; John 14:12; Romans 5:1-2;
2 Cor. 5:7; James 2:5; James 5:15; Rev. 2:19; Psalm 68:19;
Galatians 6:2; 1 John 4:14; Matthew 16:2-3; Matthew 24:29-30;
Mark 13:25; Rev. 17:14; Rev. 19:16

Have you ever heard the statement, *"I've got a long way to go and a short time to get there"*? That's the way life is. When we are children we ask, *"Will I ever get out of school? Will I ever get a job? Will I ever get married? Will I ever get the kids raised? Will I ever retire so I can enjoy life?"* Most of us are like the kids in the back seat asking, *"Are we there yet?"* We are wishing our life away when we say, *"I wish Friday would get here so I could get paid."* We spend too much time worrying about our economic security and not about our spiritual side of life. If we spent more time taking care of the spiritual things, the economy would straighten out on its own. We need to spend more time working for our Lord and Savior, Jesus Christ. I know that we have to make a living to take care of our family. Jesus said, *"If you don't work you don't eat."* The problem in most cases is that we want for more than we need. When my friends and I hiked the Appalachian Mountains, we learned quickly that there were a lot of things we did not need. Our wants or even what we thought we needed became a burden instead of a help. We left food at a campsite in hopes that someone else could use it because we had too much. Other hikers had left pots and pans and other things that they found were useless to them on the trail. When we burden ourselves with the things of this world we become useless in the work of the Lord. Satan becomes the master when he burdens us down with things of this world that hinder us from doing the work of the Lord. We must seek the Lord and the things He provides so we can do His work.

11

JESUS

Jesus, the wonderful Savior, He hears my every plea.
Jesus, the wonderful Savior, from sin He set me free.
He is the wonderful Savior; He is the Shepherd too.
He is the wonderful Savior; to Him I will be true.

He leads me to still waters; He gives me waters pure.
He leads me to green pastures making my pathway sure.
He leads me over the mountains; the pathway is so steep.
He leads me through the valleys giving me restful sleep.

He feeds me with His manna, the word it is so sweet.
He rescues me from danger, my soul He doth keep.
He directs and protects me with His staff and rod.
He is my Lord and Savior; He is my Holy God.

He is the loving Shepherd; He wants to show the way.
He is the loving Savior, please come to Him today.

January 2001

Psalm 25:5; Isaiah 19:20; Isaiah 43:11; Luke 2:11; John 4:42; Acts 5:31;
2 Tim. 1:10; Titus 2:13; Psalm 55:17; Psalm 145:19; 1 John 5:14-15;
Hebrews 10:22; Psalm 23:2; Proverbs 12:28; Psalm 104:8; Psalm 104:10;
Jeremiah 31:26; Daniel 12:2; 1 Thes. 4:14; Deut. 8:16; Neh. 9:20;
John 6:31; John 6:58; Rev. 2:17; Micah 7:14; Jeremiah 48:17

Jesus guides us in truth and teaches us by His words. He hears our distress call and comes to our aid. When we reverence Him, He meets our needs and supplies us with the things that will help us grow spiritually. I mentioned earlier that when we had goats I had to get a young kid out of a fence where he had gotten hung up. Goats are much like sheep except maybe a little more hardheaded, as daddy used to say. They have to be taken care of or they will get into trouble. They have to be watered and fed. They have to be taken care of when sick or injured. God provides all of what the animals He created needs to survive, but He also put man here to take care of the animals. Just as the farmer takes care of the animals in his charge, God takes care of us. The Bible tells us that God uses His staff and rod, not to harm us, but to protect us from our enemy who comes to rob and kill us. Who is this enemy? Too many times we think that our enemy is the one who steals from us or tries to do us harm, but they have the same enemy as we do. Satan is the enemy of all mankind. Jesus says in John 10:10, *"The thief comes only to steal and kill and destroy; I have come that they may have life, and have it to the full."*
If we follow the ways of Satan, he will destroy you. He is not your friend. You've heard the saying, *"The enemy of my enemy is my friend."* Satan is definitely not our friend. He is the worst enemy we will ever have. Jesus is the only way because He is the Son of God and He gave His life for us on the cross that we will have life if we believe in Him. He gives us manna from heaven (the word of God) and living water that cleanses us of our sins and gives us eternal life. He is the Good Shepherd who takes care of us.

12

FISHING

I want to go a fishing to catch some fish you see.
I want to go a fishing to catch some fish for me.
And when I go a fishing, I carry all kinds of bait.
And when I go a fishing, I don't like to be too late.

And when I go a fishing, I like to be well prepared.
And when I go a fishing, I don't like to be deterred.
And when I go a fishing, I take my rod, reel and pole.
And when I go a fishing, sometimes I like to troll.

There's another kind of fishing, I have been taught.
Of the Lord Jesus Christ and all the souls He's caught.
I'd like to go a fishing to catch some souls for Him.
But when I fish for souls of men, I have a lamp to trim.

I get my bait, pole and tackle and listen for his call.
I set my mind upon God's word so I might not slip and fall.
My pole's the Holy Spirit that extends far out to reach
The hearts of men so far away, God's truths to teach.

My tackle is the Word of God that works in a wondrous way,
To keep the hearts of men on track, that they might never stray.
For bait, I use peace, love and joy to catch the souls of men,
And when they're caught for Jesus, He sets them free again.

February 1993

Matthew 4:18-19; Matthew 13:47; Mark 1:16-17; Luke 5:5-6; Luke
5:10; John 21:6; John 21:8; John 21:11

Uncle J D Williams

In Matthew 4:19, Jesus said, *"Come follow me and I will make you fishers of men."* I could tell you many fish stories, but in this space I only have room for one. My brother, Billy, and I fished in the Ocmulgee River just below Abbeville, Georgia, around Rhodes Lake. On one occasion, we were pitching crickets for anything that would bite. For this we used a small pole with nothing but a line and hook and light sinker and, of course, the bait (cricket). We would troll up the river pitching our crickets into the slow moving water along the banks of the river where limbs or trees had fallen. Billy spotted where two limbs had formed a triangle next to the bank leaving a small opening about 20 inches. He pitched his cricket in and wham, he pulls up a large bluegill. He baits his hook again and looks at me. I asked, *"Are you going to catch another one in the same spot?"* He pitches the cricket into the triangle and wham, up comes a two-pound bass. How he got him in the boat I'll never know. If you catch fish you have to go where the fish are and you have to be a fisherman. You can't just sit around the house, fill the sink with water and expect the fish to jump in. You have to go where the fish are. Jesus called us to be fishers of men. What He was saying was that we were to be witnesses for His kingdom. We are to go into the highways and byways and tell folks about the love of our Lord Jesus. For God so loved the world that He sent Jesus, His only Son, as a sacrifice for our sins. When we come to Jesus willingly confessing our sins, He forgives us and cleans us up, then He sets us free to enjoy life; a life of peace, joy and love. A life filled with spiritual blessings far greater than anything we will gain by following Satan.

13

FALLOW GROUND

Have you plowed your field today,
Have you cleared away the stubble?
Have you plowed your field today,
Have you taken time and trouble?

Have you prepared fallow ground,
To receive those precious seeds?
Have you seized the time today,
To meet someone's special needs?

Our lives become so cluttered,
With the things of this world.
We're always running to and fro,
Our lives are always in a swirl.

We need to take the time to weed,
Those garden spots of our life.
Give the word a chance to grow,
And take away the worldly strife.

Take the time to clear the ground,
Upon which your seeds may grow.
Take the time to share the word,
That the love of God might show.

February 1995

Job 4:8; Proverbs 20:4; Isaiah 28:24; 1 Cor. 9:10; Psalm 107:37;
Psalm 126:5; Hosea 10:12; Matthew 13:18-51; Isaiah 51:3; Isaiah
58:11; Isaiah 61:11; Jeremiah 31:12; Joel 2:3

Job said those who plow evil and sow trouble reap it (Job 4:8). The old saying is, *"What you sow is what you reap."* If we sow what is good we will reap good things. When we sow good seed into good soil, it will produce good fruit. God blesses us with material and spiritual blessings to use in this world, but a question needs to be asked. Can we misuse those blessings for evil? I think the answer is yes. The answer to this is in the parable of the talents in Matthew 25. Most people, when they read this parable, think of material things because the Bible does use talents to describe the value of gold and silver. Jesus was more concerned about the spiritual side since that is why He came and died for us on the cross. If we get the spiritual side corrected, then the economic side will correct itself. We can be economically well off, but without Jesus, we are doomed to eternal torment with Satan. To sow Spiritual Seeds we have to know the word of God. For seed to grow they have to be placed in soil Isaiah 61:11 says, *"For as the soil makes the sprout come up and a garden causes seeds to grow, so the Sovereign Lord will make righteousness and praise spring up before all nations."*

I've seen some so called preachers spend all their time asking for money and never telling anyone about Jesus. Isaiah 28:24 says, *"When a farmer plows for planting, does he plow continually? Does he keep on breaking up and harrowing the soil?"*

When we do this the soil will dry up and blow away and there will be no harvest of souls for Jesus, but when we plant the seeds God gives us and look to Him we will see great things. Isaiah 51:3 states, *"The Lord will surely comfort Zion and will look with compassion on all her ruins; he will make her deserts like Eden, her wastelands like the garden of the Lord. Joy and gladness will be found in her, thanksgiving and the sound of singing.*

14

Fallow Ground

"If you will return to me O Israel and put your abominations out of my sight then you shall not be removed. If you swear that the Lord lives in truth, judgment, and righteousness and by Him the nations shall bless themselves and in Him they will glory. Then the Lord will say to you, "Break up your fallow ground and do not plant among the thorns. Circumcise your hearts to the Lord so my fury will not come like fire so that none can quench it because of your evil ways." Jeremiah 4:1-4

When daddy cleared new ground so he could plant the seed, it took a lot of hard work. He did not have the money to hire bulldozers to clear away the trees and stumps. He had to pull up what he could with a **B John Deere** tractor. He would dig around some of them and cut the feed roots so that the main trunk and taproot could be removed from the ground. He would use dynamite on the real tough ones and send them sailing high into the air.

All the stumps, limbs, and debris were placed in large piles and burned. Everything possible was done to remove anything that would hinder the planting, but even then, there were those things that would try to take the land. There were weeds, thorns, and roots that would sprout and choke out the desired plant. The field had to be plowed and cultivated so the seed that were planted could grow under the best possible conditions. Then it could produce fruit that could be harvested that was good for the people.

After daddy had cleared the field and planted the seed, which in this case was black diamond watermelons, he still had to work hard to keep the weeds out. This meant plowing with that same **B John Deere** tractor and hand pulling and hoeing or cutting the weeds out by the roots. Then fertilizer, or as some would say guano, had to be applied to the crop to give it the nutrients it needed to produce good fruit. Then there were many prayers that God would send the rains and bless the crop, and He did. Those watermelons would average thirty pounds, and one of the largest weighed almost eighty pounds.

The crop was good and the melons were sweet but then came the harvesting and marketing. Daddy arranged for two trucks to take those melons to the farmer's market in Atlanta. The two truck drivers, daddy and I took off for the big city. We did not see much of the city, just the farmer's market, a local restaurant and a bakery. The market was flooded with watermelons and no one was buying. We started out at a dollar apiece, but after ten days, we decided we wanted to get rid of those melons and go home. Some boys came by in a pickup truck and asked what we would take for the melons if they bought a truckload. I had talked to daddy and he agreed to let those boys have the watermelon for fifteen cents apiece. We did not know if they would be back but they were soon back for another load. They knew where to get rid of those melons. Soon we were on our way home and boy, was I glad. We loaded some onto our old pickup and took them to nearby towns and sold a few more. We took two loads to the prison camp near Workmore and gave them to the prisoners. Daddy believed it was better to give something away than let it rot in the field.

15

EVERLASTING LIGHT

There's an everlasting light in my life.
There's an everlasting light in my life.
There's an everlasting light,
And it shines both day and night.
There's an everlasting light in my life.

There's an everlasting love in my heart.
There's an everlasting love in my heart.
There's an everlasting love,
And it comes from above.
There's an everlasting love in my heart.

There's an everlasting life in my soul.
There's an everlasting life in my soul.
There's an everlasting life,
And it comes from Jesus Christ.
There's an everlasting life in my soul.

There's an everlasting joy in my heart.
There's an everlasting joy in my heart.
There's an everlasting joy,
Brought by Christ, the baby boy.
There's an everlasting joy in my heart.

There's an everlasting balm in my soul.
There's an everlasting balm in my soul.
There's an everlasting balm,
And it brings peace and calm.
There's an everlasting balm in my soul.

Feb. 1995

Genesis 9:16; Psalm 90:2; Jeremiah 10:10; Ezekiel 37:26; Daniel 12:2;
John 3:16; John 5:24; Romans 6:22; 1 Tim. 6:16; Jeremiah 33:11;
Matthew 13:20; Matthew 25:21; Luke6:23 ; Acts 20:24; Philemon 1:7;
1 John 1:4; Luke 1:79; Luke 2:14; John 16:33; Romans 14:17; Romans
15:13

There was an old oak tree in the front yard of the house where I grew up. I believe that tree could have been there when Columbus discovered America. I played under that tree from the time I could walk until my teenage years. They say that trees of that type can live 500 years or more. There was a beginning and ending to that old tree because that's the way life is in this world. Everlasting things belong to God and are spiritual in nature because God is eternal. We can have these eternal blessings from God when we accept His Son, Jesus, as our Savior. The first everlasting blessing is the light that comes from Jesus. He is the true light that takes the darkness of sin out of our lives.

John 1:6-9 says, *"There came a man who was sent from God; his name was John. He came as a witness to testify concerning that light, so that through him all men might believe. He, himself, was not the light; he came only as a witness to the light. The true light that gives light to every man was coming into the world."*

Because of the light that Jesus brings to us, we also have eternal life. John 3:16 says, *For God so loved the world that he gave his one and only Son, that whoever believes in him shall not perish but have eternal life."*

John 5:24: *"I tell you the truth, whoever hears my word and believes him who sent me has eternal life and will not be condemned; he has crossed over from death to life."*

Because Jesus came to give us life, we have love, joy and peace in our lives. All these things can be eternal if we accept Jesus as our Savior. Confessing our sins to Him and Him only, we are forgiven of all we have done to Him, to ourselves, and to others. This is His everlasting covenant with us. He has also made an everlasting covenant with Israel and we will discuss this later.

16

DAY TO DAY

Walk with God from day to day,
And He will always show the way.

Seek His will in all you do,
And He will always be so true.

He will lift you high above,
And let you soar like a dove.

Seek His will from day to day,
And He will always show the way.

October 1994

Psalm 25:8; Psalm 25:12; Proverbs 4:11; Jeremiah 42:3; Matthew 3:3; Genesis 5:22; Genesis 5:24; Genesis 6:9; 1 Chron. 12:22; Luke 11:3; 2 Cor. 4:16; Job 5:8; Amos 5:8; Matthew 6:33; Matthew 7:7; Matthew 28:5; Acts 17:27; Col. 3:1

John David Harrell 1983

Genesis 5:24 says that Enoch walked with God and was no more because God took him away. Enoch had to be a very righteous man for God to have taken him away before the flood. His son, Methuselah, died just days before the flood. Do not get this Enoch mixed up with the son of Cain named Enoch in Genesis 4. We know that this Enoch of Chapter 5 was translated or taken away by God because of his faith and testimony and he pleased God (Hebrew 11:5). We know that Enoch was also a prophet of God. In Jude 14, it states that he prophesied that God was coming with His saints to judge those that were ungodly. All we know about Methuselah is that he lived longer than any man we know (969 years) and he died before the flood, yet more people know about Methuselah than Enoch. I believe that Methuselah was a godly man also and went to Heaven to be with the Lord. I do not even claim to be close to either of these men in my righteousness. The question should be asked, *"Are we just trying to live a long life in this world, or are we truly walking with the Lord as best we can with what time we have?"* It was not easy in Noah's day to live a righteous life, but if Noah had not obeyed God mankind would have ended there. We must allow God to instruct us in His ways for He is the way. John 14:6: *Jesus answered, 'I am the way and the truth and the life. No one comes to the Father except through me.'* He will instruct us in the ways of wisdom that will lead us along straight paths to a life more wonderful than anything we have ever known (Proverbs 4:11). God has marked the trail well, not only with His words, but with the blood of His son, Jesus, who gave His life on the cross that we might have eternal life. Accept His love today. It is freely given, not forced upon us.

17

DEAR LORD

This life I live, my dear Lord, I give it now to thee.
For by the cross, my dear Lord, you gave your life for me

This life I live, my dear Lord, is but an empty shell.
But by your death, my dear Lord, it was spared from hell.

This life I live, my dear Lord, is weak from worldly sin.
By your strength, my dear Lord, I can overcome again.

When I accept you, my dear Lord, you come and set me free.
You give so much, my dear Lord, you gave your life for me.

December 1992

Matthew 4:4; Matthew 4:10; Matthew 5:33; Matthew 7:21;
Matthew 8:2; Matthew 9:38; Matthew 10:38; Matthew 16:24;
Matthew 20:8; Matthew 23:39; Matthew 24:42;
Matthew 24:45-46; Matthew 25:44; Matthew 28:6;
Matthew 9:18; Acts 2:28; Acts 11:18; Acts 20:24

When we first started going to the north Georgia mountains, I knew very little about the Appalachian Trail, but once I found out about it I knew that it had to be a part of my life. It is that way when you get to know Jesus and learn what He did and is doing for you. He fills that empty space in your life the way nothing else can. It is what He did and what He is doing for us that makes life worthwhile. Many are looking for something to fill that empty spot. It may be a job or money and then alcohol or drugs, but this is like trying to put a square peg in a round hole. There is only one thing that will fill that space and that is the love of Jesus. We are made in the image of God, therefore, He must take His place in our lives and give us true life. In Acts 20:24, Paul said he must finish the race with joy and complete the task that Jesus had given him. We all have a task before us that we accomplish, but we can only succeed if we trust the Lord to give us strength to do so. As I sit here writing this, I'm thinking that it looks like I will never get finished, because my mind is on other things less important. It seems that worldly things creep in and distract us from our true task. Sure, there are other things that have to be done and time has to be set aside for those things, but testifying to the gospel must come first. Many of us are like the actors in the movies when they are in a race. We are always looking to see who is about to catch up with us and we try to stop them with some kind of trap or roadblock. When we do this, we only get further behind and we take our eyes off the goal. It does not matter who is ahead or behind if we run for Christ because we all win when we allow Jesus to be first in our lives. Does Jesus come first in your life? Do you pray for His guidance each day? If not, accept Him into your heart today.

18

THE CUP

When Jesus comes into our lives, His work, His work's not done.
When Jesus comes into our lives, His work has just begun.
He sends His Holy Spirit into our lives, to fill, to fill our cup.
He sends His Holy Spirit into our lives, to lift, to lift us up.

That cup He gives we must share, this day, this very day.
That cup He gives we must share, along, along life's way.
That cup's a blessing to us all, it gives, it gives us strength.
That cup's a blessing to us all, to God, to God give thanks.

I've seen the Lamb of God coming down from above.
I've seen the Lamb of God with His pure love.
I've seen the Lamb of God coming down from above,
Like a snow white dove.

Each time we share from this cup, He doth, He doth refill.
Each time we share from this cup, we do, we do His will.
The love of God must be shared, it's every, everywhere.
The love of God must be shared, if we, if we do care.

When Jesus comes into our lives, His work, His work's not done.
When Jesus comes into our lives, we've just, we've just begun.
For the work Jesus gives us, He gives us strength each day.
For the work Jesus gives us, He shows us the way.

I've seen the Lamb of God coming down from above.
I've seen the Lamb of God with His pure love.
I've seen the Lamb of God coming down from above,
Like a snow white dove.

September 1992

Genesis 44:17; 2 Samuel 12:3; Psalm 16:5; Psalm 23:5;
Psalm 73:10; Psalm 116:13; Matthew 10:42; Matthew 20:22-23;
Matthew 26:27; Matthew 26:39; Luke 22:20; 1 Cor. 10:16;
1 Cor. 10:21; Psalm 111:3; Proverbs 16:11; John 9:4;
Philip. 1:6; 1 Thess. 4:11; 1 Tim. 3:1; Hebrews 6:10; Rev. 22:12

Before Jesus faced the trial and crucifixion, He went to an upper room of a friend to serve the Passover meal to His disciples. There He would institute the Lord's Supper. The Passover began in Egypt when God delivered the Hebrew people from bondage. God sent ten plagues upon Egypt to convince Pharaoh to let His people go. The tenth plague was the death of every first born in Egypt, but the Hebrew children would be spared by obeying God. God commanded the Israelites to prepare a meal which would become the Passover. This meal was more than something to give them physical strength to make the journey they had to make, but it would also show their faith in God to deliver them from their enemy (Exodus 12). When jesus and the disciples met in the upper room, they observed the Passover just as they did in Egypt as God had commanded them to do. Then Jesus took the wine and unleavened bread and gave it to His disciples. He was about to become their Passover lamb because He was the Lamb of God and He was to be sacrificed on the cross for their sins and our sins. He gave them unleavened bread which means that the sins has been taken out of our lives when we accept Him as our Lord and Savior. He also gave them wine which represented His blood that He shed when He gave His life for us on the cross.

Luke 22:20: *"In the same way, after the supper he took the cup, saying, 'This cup is the new covenant in my blood, which is poured out for you.'"*

The cup that Jesus gave His disciples and to us is a cup of joy, truth and righteousness, but the cup that He drank was a bitter cup of our sins. Matthew 26:39: *"Going a little farther, he fell with his face to the ground and prayed, 'My Father, if it is possible, may this cup be taken from me. Yet not as I will, but as you will.'"*

19

THE SPIRIT

Peace like a river flows over my life,
Peace like a river flows deep.
Peace like a river flows over my life,
My soul, the Lord doth keep.

The Spirit of God flows over my life,
He gives me strength each day.
The Spirit of God flows over my life,
He desires to show me the way.

The Spirit of God lifts up my life,
He lifts me out of my sin.
The Spirit of God lifts up my life,
He teaches me how to win.

February 3, 1998

Genesis 1:2; Exodus 31:3; Numbers 11:17; 2 Samuel 23:2;
Ezekiel 18:31; Luke 11:13; John 3:5; John 4:23; Romans 8:4-5;
1 Cor.3:16; 1 Cor. 12:13; 1 Peter 1:2; 1 John 4:1-3; Rev. 19:10; Rev.
22:17; Rev. 22:1-2;Psalm 37:37; Luke 8:48; John 14:27;
1 Cor. 1:3; Philip. 4:7; 2 Tim. 2:22; 2 Peter 1:2; Rev. 1:4

I have spent many a day on the Ocmulgee River either fishing or just relaxing and enjoying the peace and tranquility of the beauty around me. The river flows south out of the north Georgia mountains through Macon and then turns east at Abbeville, Georgia, to form the southern border of Telfair County. At the present, I am only two miles from the river.

Sometimes when I would go to the river, I felt that it would wash all my cares and troubles away and they would float down the river into the ocean and never be seen again. God's Spirit comes into our lives like that river and carries not only our cares away but He cleanses us of our sins and washes them into the sea. The death of Jesus on the cross created that spiritual river in our lives to give us new life. There are many troubles in this life, but we can have peace in our lives if we trust in Christ and allow Him to live in our hearts. We are to live according to the Spirit of God and not according to the sinful nature we are born with that leads us down the wrong path. If we live according to the sinful nature, we seek the sinful things of this world and that leads to trouble, but if we seek the spiritual things of God, we will have peace, joy and love.

I John 4 says that we are not to believe every spirit but to test the spirits. There are many false or evil spirits but there is only one spirit of God, that is the Holy Spirit. There were those in the early church that were teaching false doctrine. They were mixing the true teachings of Jesus with their own doctrine and believers were confused because they were not grounded in the true word of God. When Jesus went to be with the Father to take His rightful place, He sent the Holy Spirit to comfort and teach us the truth of God's word and live by the Spirit. Will we understand everything in the Bible? Absolutely not! Learning is a growing process and we will still be learning in Heaven.

20

TALENTS

How do we use our talents God gives us every day?
How do we use our talents----Do we stop and pray?
Do we ask the Lord for guidance in all that we do?
Do we ask the Lord for guidance and try to be true?

Do we use our talents and serve the Lord with glee,
Or do we use our talents for all the world to see?
For if we use our talents for our Lord up above,
We show to all the world the nature of His love.

May 5, 1998

1 Cor. 12:1; 1 Cor. 12:4; 1 Cor. 12:9; 1 Cor. 12:28; 1 Cor. 14:1;
1 Cor. 14:12; Romans 15:6; 1 Peter 2:12; 1 Peter 4:16;
Matthew 6:3

When we use the word talent, sometimes we get confused in our interpretation of what it means, especially when we read the parable in Matthew 25 about the servants who were given the talents and used them to produce more talents. We think of the saying, *"It takes money to make money."* Even in this parable I believe Jesus is talking more about the abilities God gives us through the Holy Spirit so we might serve him. All talents or gifts come from God, but this does not mean that we always use those gifts in the right way. The "parable of the talents" was spoken still further to illustrate the manner in which he would deal with people at his return to judgment. The words "the kingdom of heaven" are not in the original, but are very properly inserted by the translators. The design of the parable is to teach that those who improve their talents or faculties in the cause of religion, who improve them to their own salvation, and in doing good to others, shall be proportionally rewarded; but they who neglect their talents, and who neither secure their own salvation, nor do good to others, will be punished. The kingdom of heaven is like such a man – that is, *"God deals with people in his government as such a man did"* (Albert Barnes Commentary on the Bible). God gives us our talents, but it is up to us to decide how we will use them. Will we use them for God or to gain worldly fame?

21

THE LIGHT

Jesus is the light that shines down from above,
And shows to all mankind the way to perfect love.

Jesus is the light that comes into our heart,
And brightens every corner nevermore to depart.

Jesus is the light that gives life to a dying soul,
If we'll only ask Him to come and take control.

September 2000

Exodus 25:6; Exodus 25:37; Leviticus 24:2; Job 22:28; Job 33:28;
Job 33:30; Job 37:21; Psalm 43:3; Psalm 97:11; Proverbs 13:9;
Matthew 6:22; Luke 11:36; John 8:12; John 9:5; John 12:46;
Rev. 22:5; Acts 1:5

Light is the most important resource in God's creation. If it were not for light there would not be any life. The Bible says that in the beginning the world was dark and void. After the world was created, God put the sun in its place, then life could be put here. Astronomers say that if the earth were just a fraction of the distance closer to the sun, we would burn to a crisp. If we were a fraction of the distance away from the sun we would freeze into a ball of ice. I'm glad we have a creator who knows what He is doing. There are many other factors that come into play so that life can be on planet earth, such as rotation, tilt, and movement around the sun.

Yes, mankind can live on earth for a number of years and enjoy what God put here. He can have a good life if he takes care of himself, but the life we live now will have to end at some point. What about after that? Is there life after death? Does it matter what we believe? God not only gave us the sun, but He gave us HIS son who came to give us spiritual life. There is a type of darkness that fills the earth twenty four hours a day and it's that darkness that separates us from the love of God. That darkness is caused by sin. We all have sinned and come short of the glory of God. Because of the sin in our lives, we have spiritual darkness in our lives, but when we ask Jesus to come into lives, we are born again and we truly have eternal life. When this happens the Holy Spirit enters our hearts and we become members of God's family. Accept Christ today and thank God for His Son who shed His blood so we might have a new life.

22

WHAT HAVE I DONE?

What have I done to deserve the love that God gives to me?
What have I done to deserve the love that is given so free?
What have I done to deserve the beauty I see along the way?
What have I done to deserve the beauty that blesses every day?

What have I done to deserve the blessings God sends from above?
What have I done to deserve the blessings that tell of His love?
What have I done to deserve the life that burns within my soul?
What have I done to deserve the life more precious than gold?

What have I done to deserve the freedom to live the life I do?
What have I done to deserve the freedom to serve a God so true?
What have I done, my precious Lord, to deserve anything you give?
You gave your life, my precious Lord that I might learn to live.

December 1992

Ezra 9:13-15; Romans 5:5; Romans 8:39; 2 Cor. 13:14;
2 Thes. 3:5; Titus 3:4-5; 1 John 2:5; 1 John 3:16-17; 1 John 4:9;
1 John 5:3; Jude 1:21; Psalm 27:4; Psalm 45:11; Psalm 50:2;
Psalm 90:17; Psalm 96:6; Psalm 96:9; Isaiah 33:17; Proverbs 10:22; Isaiah 44:3; Ezekiel 34:26;
Malachi 3:10; Rev. 7:12; Acts 22:28

HOLY SPIRIT

The Holy Spirit of our Lord comes to give us strength.
In all we say and do and live to God, we do give thanks.
The Holy Spirit of our Lord comes to give us love.
He comes to us from heaven like a swooping mourning dove.

The Holy Spirit of our Lord comes to give us peace and rest.
He comes into our hearts and lives to help us pass the test.
The Holy Spirit of our Lord comes to give grace and reprieve.
He came to remind us how Jesus, our sins He did relieve.

The Holy Spirit of our Lord comes to give us heavenly power,
That all might come to know of Christ and see His shining tower.
The Holy Spirit of our Lord comes to give His comfort to us,
That we might come to know the Lord and in Him put our trust.

The Holy Spirit of our Lord comes to give us time,
That we might do the things God places in our mind.

July 5, 1995

Psalm 51:11; Luke 11:13; Ephes. 1:13; Ephes. 4:30; 1 Thes. 4:8;
Isaiah 33:6; Jeremiah 16:19; Hosea 12:3; Mark 12:30; Acts 9:22;
2 Cor. 12:9; Rev. 3:8; Rev. 12:10; 2 Samuel 22:3; 2 Samuel 22:51; Psalm 61:3; Psalm 144:2;
Proverbs 18:10; Psalm 59:16; Mark 9:1; Luke 1:35; Acts 1:7-8; Acts 4:33; Romans 1:16;
Rev. 2:26; Job 35:14; Psalm 18:30; Psalm 25:20

THE STAR

Behold the star of Bethlehem; it comes to show the way.
Behold the town of Bethlehem where the Christ child lay.

Do you see the star shining so brightly in the sky?
The wise men saw it shining and asked the reason why.
The star shone so brightly to lead the wise men there,
To the town of Bethlehem where the child slept so fair.

To Him they gave great riches, gold, frankincense, and myrrh.
He brought the love of God to men their hearts to stir.
So in this world of sin and dark look for the star so bright,
That brings to us that shining love of God's own holy light.

November 1995

Numbers 24:17; Matthew 2:7; Matthew 2:7; Matthew 2:9-10; 2 Peter 1:19;
Rev. 2:28; Rev. 22:16; Micah 5:2; Matthew 2:1; Matthew 2:5-6; Matthew 2:8; Matthew 2:16;
Luke 2:4; Luke 2:15; John 7:42; Isaiah 50:10; Isaiah 58:8;
Isaiah 60:3; Isaiah 60:19; Daniel 2:22; Matthew 10:27; Luke 1:79; Luke 8:16;
John 5:35; Acts 26:18; 1 Peter 2:9; Rev. 22:5

PEACE, LOVE AND JOY

Peace, love and joy come to us at Christmas time.
Peace, love and joy ring out the Christmas chime.
May peace come to your heart every day of the year.
May each day of your life be filled with good cheer.

The peace that comes from Christ is the best of all.
Just open up your heart and hear the Master's call.
The love that comes from Christ is so freely given.
It showers down upon man from every part of Heaven.

We give that love to others and show that we care.
We reach out to others that precious love to share.
The love that comes from Christ lifts our soul high,
To strengthen us to face the day while others sigh.

Joy through the Holy Spirit gives strength each day
That we might show to others the true Christian way.

December 1994

Deut. 6:5; Deut. 7:7; Deut. 7:9; Psalm 42:4; Psalm 43:4; Psalm 97:10; Matthew 6:24; John
14:21; John 14:23; John 16:24; John 17:26; Acts 13:52; Romans 8:6;
Romans 12:9-10; 1 Peter 5:14; 1 Cor. 12:25; Luke 10:34-35; 1 Peter 5:7

26

CHRISTMAS

May the Christmas spirit come to you and give you joy.
May you experience peace through Christ, the baby boy.

For He did come into the world to give peace to man,
And He can give eternal life, if with Him you stand.

Jesus was the Christ child born on Christmas day.
Jesus was the Christ child, the star showed the way.

Jesus was the Christ child who came to give us joy.
Jesus was the Christ child, God's own baby boy.

December 1998

Luke 1:35; Luke 4:3; Luke 4:9; John 1:49; John 3:18; John 5:25; John 11:4; John 20:31;
Romans 1:4; Galatians 2:20; Ephes. 4:13; Hebrews 4:14; Hebrews 7:3;
1 John 3:8; 1 John 5:10; 1 John 5:20; Rev. 2:18

PEACE

May the joy of Christmas be yours this day,
And may the peace of Christ come your way.
In the times of troubles, we have true joy,
As we seek the Messiah, the little baby boy.

In Him is found true peace not found by man,
Until our lives are touched by His holy hand.
As we reach out to others to share His love,
We give the peace that comes only from above.

He touched the hearts of men with words true,
Now He is touching others by using me and you.
He gave us many blessings throughout the year,
Let us give to others---- Peace, Love and Cheer.

December 1993

Daniel 9:25-26; Hebrews 9:28; Hebrews 10:16-18; Hebrews 13:20-21; Psalm 25:17; Psalm 34:6; Psalm 34:17; Isaiah 65:16; Mark 13:8; Proverbs 28:20; Ephes. 1:3; 1 Samuel 10:26; Luke 22:51; Luke 8:46-47; Mark 6:56; Mark 1:41

GOD COMES TO US

God comes to encourage us in many, many ways.
When we are discouraged and face the long, long days.
He comes in the form of a raven swooping down from above.
He comes in the form of sunshine to share His perfect love.

He comes in the form of a cloud to bring us the rain.
He comes to the blind and cripple in the form of a cane.
He comes in the form of a tree to give shade to you and me.
He comes in the form of a child to set men free.

He comes in the form of a flower to give beauty to our eyes.
He comes in the form of stars to light up the night skies.
He comes in the form of a friend to share our troubles with.
He comes in the form of dew in the early morning mist.

He comes in the form of a mountain to bring trials to our life.
That we might gain strength in a world filled with strife.

March 1995

Deut. 1:38; 2 Samuel 11:25; Gen. 8:7; Gen. 9:13; Ex. 13:21; Gen.18:4; Mat. 18:4-5;
2 Tim. 3:15; Ex. 33:11; Num. 11:9

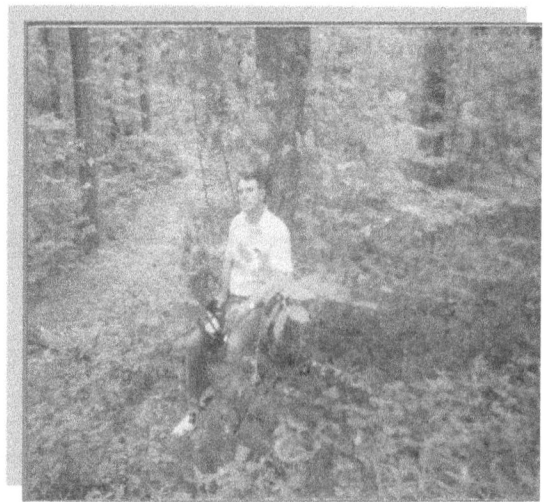

THE PRODIGAL SON

The prodigal son came home that day,
To a father that forgave his sinful way.
He went away with sin in his heart.
When he came back that sin did depart.

He went away to the ways of the world.
Money in his pocket, his life in a swirl.
He wound up in a pigpen eating cornhusk.
His soul had grown weary covered with dust.

He was hungry, tired and just plain worn out.
His friends deserted him and he begins to pout.
His heart grew weary from such a heavy load,
So he begins to walk up a long dusty road.

Walking down that road, he thought about home.
He wanted to go there nevermore to roam.
He thought about his father, what would he say?
Would he forgive him of his sinful way?

Walking down that road he thought, what was left?
He would become a servant and not think of himself.
As he traveled down that long dusty road,
His heart was changed, carrying a lighter load.

When he approached home, his father at the gate,
Had he changed in time or was he too late?
His father met him with arms open wide.
When the son saw him, he picked up his stride.

They hugged and cried with tears flowing down.
It was time for a party with friends all around.
God is our father and He loves us so much.
He wants to renew us with His precious touch.

He loved us so much that Jesus He sent,
To die on the cross if we will repent.
If we turn from our sins, He will welcome us home,
To a place that is called heaven, nevermore to roam.
October 2005
Luke 15:6; Psalm 16:5-6; Eccles. 11:9; Luke 15:11-32; Isaiah 55:2; Jeremiah 31:19; Psalm 84:10;
Isaiah 61:10; Rev. 3:18; John 5:24-25; Deut. 30:2-4; Job 33:27-28

THANK GOD FOR MOUNTAINS

The mountains of north Georgia are there for all to see.
They rise above the landscape as tall as can be.
They stand there so tall to challenge body and mind.
They give us beauty and strength if we take the time.

When we climb a mountain, it builds our body and soul.
When we climb a mountain, our Spirit grows more bold.
The mountains in our life are trials we face each day.
They come into our lives to challenge along life's way.

Jesus faced the ultimate trial and died upon the cross.
He suffered so much for us; He died to save the lost.
Jesus died on a mountain for the entire world to see.
Jesus died on a mountain called Mount Calvary.

Thank God for mountains that come into our life.
They help give us strength to overcome our strife.
Thank God for our Savior who died on the cross.
Thank God for our Savior who died to save the lost.

November 17, 2005

Luke 23:33; Matthew 27:33-34; John 19:17-18; Mark 15:22-23; Hebrews 13:12-13;
Zech. 12:10; Matthew 20:19; Mark 10:33-34; 1 Peter 2:24; Romans 7:25;
Psalm 21:13; Isaiah 26:4; Romans 5:6; Rev. 5:12; Rev. 12:10

31

THE SOWER

The sower sowed his seed, they fell on fallow ground.
The sower sowed his seed, they scattered all around.
The seed were very good, they came from God above.
The seed were very good, the fruit from God's love.

Some fell on thorny hearts, their life was choked out.
Seed cannot produce fruit when people begin to doubt.
Some fell on stony hearts where they spring up, but died.
While having no soil to grow upon, the word was denied.

Some fell by the wayside, some said it wouldn't matter.
When the word was not preached they began to scatter.
When some fell on good soil where they began to grow,
They began to prosper, the love of God began to show.

Let our hearts be good soil so God can plant His seed.
Then we can produce the fruit the world really needs.
God's word is the seed that's planted in our hearts.
The seed is so very good, all it needs is a place to start.

December 23, 2005

Jeremiah 4:3; Hosea 10:12; Genesis 3:18; Matthew 13:1-23: Mark 4:18-19; Galatians 6:7-8;
Isaiah 28:23-25; Luke 8:15; Matthew 15:13

THE BLOSSOMING DESERT

I walked through the desert, so desolate and bare.
Not a drop of rain, no water was found there.
No life was found on this parched piece of soil.
No one to live there, no one to work and toil.

This land belonged to God, yet it had no life.
It was harsh and barren, and so full of strife.
It seemed God had left the land, the sun bore down.
Anything that sprang to life soon turned brown.

Then God called His people to return to the land.
They would return to Israel, there to make a stand.
It would not be easy; there would be toil and strife.
By trusting in their God, there would spring new life.

Then water came from the ground at the hand of God,
Turning the desert into a place of very fertile sod.
The desert began to blossom and bring forth life anew.
And once again the word of God was proven to be true.

Then from the desert ground came a refreshing pool.
The water was so pure and to the touch so cool.
Through the parched desert there ran a great highway.
The precious children of God had come home to stay.

God called His people to work the fallow ground.
They began to work the soil, and life was all around.
Dates, Figs and all things that man enjoys so much.
They all spring from the ground at the Master's touch.

Our lives are so dry and barren until our God above,
Reaches down to touch us with His eternal love.
He fills us with bubbling water that gives eternal life.
He takes away our sin and helps us deal with strife.

He sent His son, Christ Jesus, to die upon the cross.
To give new life to all men, He came to save the lost.
If you desire to have new life then Jesus is the way.
Don't wait another minute, please come to Him today.
Feb. 20, 2006
Isaiah 35; Psalm 63:1; Isaiah 32:2; Isaiah 32:15-16; Isaiah 35:6;
Jeremiah 4:3; Hosea 10:12

SAVIOR

Jesus is our Savior, He gives us loving care.
The suffering He went through we cannot bear.
Beaten without mercy and nailed to the cross.
He suffered so much, He surely paid the cost.

He gives bread and milk that is free for you and me,
For He paid the price when He died on Calvary.
He is King of kings but wore a crown of thorns.
He came to show love but was treated with scorn.

The scars that He bore were for you and me.
The pain that He bore was far beyond degree.
Freedom is not free, but the cost you will find,
Has been paid by the Savior, for He's more than kind.

Kindness can help us feel good and lift our spirits up.
But kindness cannot save, He must drink from the cup.
We cannot drink from the cup, He must drink alone.
Then by faith we accept Him and our sins are gone.

He died for our sins and took away our guilt.
He made a place in heaven, mansions He has built.
One day we will go there evermore to live,
For He died on the cross, eternal life to give.

May 11, 2006

Isaiah 55; Job 36:15; Psalm 22:24; Psalm 55:3; Isaiah 53; Matthew 4:24;
2 Thes. 1:5; 2 Tim. 1:8; 2 Tim. 1:12; Hebrews 2:10; 1 Peter 2:19; Luke 10:34-35; Isaiah 55:2;
Mark 14:22; John 6:58; 1 Cor. 5:8; Exodus 3:17; 1 Peter 2:2;
John 20:25; Acts 28:2; 2 Cor. 6:6; Ephes. 2:7; Col. 3:12; Titus 3:4; 2 Peter 1:7;
John 6:27; John 6:40

THERE'LL COME A TIME

There'll come a time when we'll see our Jesus.
There'll come a time when we'll see His face.
There'll come a time when our trials are over.
There'll come a time when we finish the race.

There'll come a time when we climb our mountain.
There'll come a time when we reach the peak.
There'll come a time when Jesus walks beside us,
For He's our strength when we are weak.

There'll come a time when we'll enter our mansion.
There'll come a time when He'll welcome us home.
There'll come a time when we'll see our Jesus.
There'll come a time when we nevermore roam.

There'll come a time when we'll call on Jesus.
There'll come a time when He answers our prayer.
There'll come a time when we need a savior.
And He'll answer because He doth care.

There'll come a time, there'll come a time.
Please call on Him when you pray.
There'll come a time, there'll come a time.
Just open your heart today.

May 29, 2006

Luke 22:58-62; Eccles. 9:11; Luke 22:28; 1 Cor. 9:24; 1 Thes. 3:3; 1 Peter 1:6; Isaiah 40:29;
1 Cor. 1:27; 2 Cor. 13:9; Psalm 64:1; Psalm 65:2; Luke 1:13;
Philip. 1:4

JOB

Job was a righteous man, he lived in the land of UZ.
But Job had an enemy and his name was Beelzebub.
Job worked very hard and was glad for what he had.
When Satan saw Job served the Lord it made him mad.

Job had ten children and he prayed for them each day.
He wanted them to follow the Lord and obey His way.
He had much livestock and servants to care for them.
When Job served the Lord he didn't do it with a whim.

When Satan had enough of going round and round,
He came to the Lord and said, "I've been up and down."
The Lord said, "Consider my servant, Job is his name."
"He serves me very well and his children do the same."

Satan said, "You've built a wall about your servant Job."
"You've given him all he needs, he lives in a fine abode."
"You've given him much wealth. Why shouldn't he be true?"
"Just take away what he has then you'll see what he'll do."

Then God said, "Do what you will but do him no hurt."
"Use all your power against him and all your demons alert."
Then Satan bid God ado and came back to this world.
He meant to do all he could to put Job's life in a swirl.

He stole all of his livestock and killed his children too.
But Job remained faithful and to his God true blue.
Then Satan returned to God and said, "What do you expect?"
"Why shouldn't he be true when you protect his neck?"

God said, "Do what you will to Job but spare his life."
"My servant, Job, does well to undergo all this strife."
Then Satan touched his body and boils begin to appear.
Then Satan thought he'd won the battle when he saw a tear.

Job's wife broke down and said, "Why don't you curse God?"
"He's taken all you have and beaten you with His rod."
But Job remained faithful, with God he was in one accord.
He came to this life with nothing, he would go trusting his Lord.

Then Job's friends came to him and gave him some advice.
The things they were saying to him were not very nice.
They accused him of doing evil and disobeying God.
Job bid them ado and wished that down the road they'd trod.

Job just kept on praying and God took away the curse.
The spell Satan had put on Job, God just put in reverse.
God blessed Job in abundance and gave him all things new.
He doubled his possessions and gave back his children too.

June 2, 2006

Job 1:1; Jeremiah 25:20; Lament. 4:21; Job 1:5; Job 1:7; Job 1:10-11; Job 1:18-19;
Job 2:4-6; Job 2:9; Job 6:15; Job 14:22; Job 15:29; Job 26:1-4; Job 42:10;
Job 42:11-17

YOU GIVE ME LIFE

When I consider what Christ did for me,
When I consider He died on Calvary,
He gave His precious life to save my soul.
He gave His life, more precious than gold.

I love you Lord, You are my King.
I love you Lord, You're my everything.
I love you Lord, you saved my soul.
I love you Lord, you're in control.

You give me hope, beyond degree.
You give me hope, and set me free.
You give me hope, beyond compare.
And delivered me from Satan's snare.

You are my king, eternally.
You give me life and set me free.
I love you Lord, You're in my heart.
I love you Lord, Nevermore depart.

You give me life and deliver from sin.
You give me life and cleanse from within.
You gave your life a ransom for my soul.
You give me life more precious than gold.

June 14, 2006

MORE THAN JUST A DREAM

I've seen the mountains, I've seen the oceans. I've seen the fertile valleys in between.
But the most beautiful vision I've ever had, has only been in my dreams.

But dreams come true if we only believe and trust in the Lord.
Obey His word and follow His commands, and walk with Him in one accord.

We can only vision the things of Heaven in our feeble mind.
But the things of Heaven are very real, and we'll see them in His time.

Walls of jasper, mansions so beautiful, gates of pearls to delight my soul.
These are just a few of the things of which the word of God has told.

Waters of life flowing from the throne, fruit bearing trees along streets of gold.
These are just a few of the things of which the word says we'll behold.

Things of such beauty, things so divine, Things made by God for our eyes to see.
Then we'll see Jesus the fairest of all. Give Him praise and bow to our knee.

Let us look upon His face so divine, far more beautiful than anything we've seen.
Then we'll behold the face of God, and know that it's more than just a dream.

August 12, 2006

Genesis 28:12; Acts 2:17; Numbers 24:6; Deut. 8:7; Psalm 104:8; Isaiah 41:18; Psalm 4:5;
Psalm 20:7; Psalm 40:3; Psalm 118:8; Hebrews 2:13; Eccles. 3:11;
Isaiah 52:1; 2 Chron. 7:14; Job 16:19; Psalm 85:11; Matthew 5:45; John 6:41;
John 15:2; Rev. 22:2

39

THE RICH MAN

The rich man came to Jesus that day,
Asking the question, "What is the way?"
Seeking new life he came to Christ
Asking the way to eternal life.

Jesus asked, "Do you follow the law?"
He said, "Yes," but still a need he saw.
He had a need deep within his heart.
What he needed was a brand new start.

Jesus said, "Come follow me."
Accept My way and be set free.
He walked away with sin in his heart.
Denying the word he did depart.

Life you'll find if you turn to Him.
Serve and be true without a whim.
Give your heart and He'll give love.
And He'll give peace from above.

Jesus will come into our life,
To take away our sin and strife.
He gives us peace and life anew.
He gives us a home in Heaven too.

December 2, 2006

2 Sam. 12:1-7; Proverbs 28:11; Mat. 19:23-24; Proverbs 21:8; Malachi 2:8;
John 14:6; Matthew 4:19; Matthew 9:9; Matthew 19:16-22; Ezekiel 18:31;
Ezekiel 36:26; Luke 12:37; Luke 16:13; John 12:26; Col. 3:24; Rev. 22:3;
Matthew 26:29 NIV; John 3:16

THE BEST

I've eaten fried chicken and tasted the best,
But my doctor said I would have to eat less.
Cornbread and butter beans cooked in fat,
Lots of good things at the table where I sat.

Turnips and ham hocks cooked by grandma.
Pork chops and lima beans cooked by grandpa.
Black eyed peas and hog jowls cooked just right.
To see me eating all these things is quite a sight.

Golden fried bacon, grits, eggs and ham.
Soft buttermilk biscuits to sop sweet jam.
All these things taste real good to me,
But to eat in moderation is the key.

My doctor has told me I have cholesterol.
To correct this problem I have to eat small.
I have to be more careful of the things I eat,
But these things aren't good without fat meat.

When we get to Heaven don't worry what we'll eat.
Everything the Lord prepares will be a real treat.
The table He sets before us will be the very best.
Then the doctor won't tell us we'll have to eat less.

March 1, 2007

Genesis 2:16-17; Genesis 3:11; Genesis 3:14; Genesis 3:17; Exodus 16:15;
Leviticus 7:23-24; Leviticus 22:6; Matthew 6:31; Matthew 9:11; Matthew 15:32; Mark 14:12;
Luke 12:19; John 6:12; 1 Cor. 5:11; 1 Cor. 10:31; Rev. 3:20; Rev. 10:9

NOAH

Noah was a good man who lived in evil times.
The world was filled with troubles and crimes.
God looked upon the earth with regret in His heart.
He had created man to serve Him from the start.

God saw that man was evil and wicked to the core.
Men turned to violence and obeyed God no more.
Men turned from God and broke every command.
God's heart was broken and justice He did demand.

He would cleanse the earth and start over again.
He would need a remnant and Noah was a friend.
Noah and his family would be a brand new start.
God would make a covenant to place in his heart.

God spoke to Noah and said, "It's about to rain."
"The people of the earth will think you're insane."
"You're to build a great big boat on dry land."
"Build it strong and sturdy according to my plan."

Noah built the boat, it took one hundred years.
Then the rain began to come like great big tears.
Then the animals did come from all around.
They got on the boat before it left the ground.

The Lord was sorrowful but He had no choice.
The people had refused to listen to His voice.
The people had rebelled and refused His love.
God's judgment had to come from Heaven above.

It rained forty days upon the face of the earth.
This was not the end, it was a brand new birth.
The great flood had come but it would go away.
The water would dry up, it would be a new day.

Noah and his family would start over again.
God had chosen Noah because he was a friend.
Are you God's friend and have you given Him your life?
He will bring you through the flood of strife.

Noah found himself on the top of a mountain.
Jesus died on Calvary and became a fountain.
Accept Him as Lord, He'll take away your strife.
He'll cleanse you with blood and give you life.

March 3, 2007

Genesis 6-9; Isaiah 54:9; Ezekiel 14:14; Ezekiel 14:20; Hebrews 11:7; 1 Peter 3:20;
2 Peter 2:5; Psalm 104:6-9; Job 11:16

43

HEAVEN

I send GOD'S message just written for you.
The word of GOD is wonderful and true.
It speaks of a Savior so wonderfully divine.
It speaks of a friend so good and kind.

He stands at the door with arms open wide.
He welcomes you home on the other side.
A place of beauty with friends all around.
A place with saints making joyful sounds.

There's no other place that I'd rather be,
For when we get there we'll truly be free.
With our new body, like Jesus' it will be.
Changed in an instant, our afflictions flee.

In this Heaven we'll live with our Lord,
With so much to do we'll never get bored.
Many fertile valleys with flowers all around.
All over GOD'S Heaven beauty doth abound.

We'll live there forever in perfect peace.
All sin and evil will come to a cease.
Jesus will teach us about true life,
Wipe away tears and take away strife.

March 17, 2008

Matthew 3:17; Matthew 4:17; Matthew 5:3; Matthew 5:10; Matthew 5:12;
Luke 15:7 & 15-18; Romans 1:18; 2 Peter 1:18; Rev. 14:13; Rev. 19:14; Rev. 21:10

WALK WITH OUR LORD

I set beside the stream flowing down the mountainside.
I spoke to my Lord and Savior and in Him, I did confide.
The stream whispered softly to me and spoke of my God.
I thought of the mountain trails where my feet had trod.

Trails that lead to mountain peaks where beauty doth abound.
Trails that lead to fertile valleys with flowers all around.
The mountains rose above like many burdens come to me,
But when I reached the top all those burdens, they did flee.

We must travel over many trails as we walk with our Lord.
But we seek to follow Jesus as we serve Him in one accord.
Trails are our training ground where God gives us strength.
We must follow in His steps so we can keep our lives in rank.

There are many dangerous trails when with our Lord we walk.
Satan will try his best to stop us, for our souls he doth stalk.
There are many dangerous pitfalls when we walk His trails.
But He will stand by our side and give us strength to prevail.

May 10, 2008

Jeremiah 17:8; Amos 5:24; Exodus 6:8; Isaiah 43:10-11; Jeremiah 1:7;
Numbers 24:6; Deut. 8:7; Psalm 104:10; Isaiah 58:6; Luke 11:46; Galatians 6:2; Psalm 23:6;
Matthew 4:19; Matthew 8:22; Mark 8:34; Psalm 30:3; Psalm 143:7; Luke 14:5; Rev. 20:1-3

TICKET TO HEAVEN

There are many beautiful places on earth to be seen.
To go and see these places would be really keen.
There are many beautiful places in heaven above.
To go to these places we need a ticket given in love.

Jesus came to this world to show His perfect love.
He left His home in heaven and His throne above.
He came to teach the word and show us the way.
He came to shape our lives and mold us like clay.

He made us into vessels to carry the word of God,
Shaping our lives so we might go where Jesus trod.
Then He gave us His holy light to show us the way,
Along this trail of darkness where men sin and stray.

He gave us the bread of life to feed the souls of men,
So their souls might be filled, never to hunger again.
He has given us eternal life by His death on the cross.
He sends the saved into the world to witness to the lost.

He gives us living water to quench the fires of hell.
He left our hearts burning, for the gospel we must tell.
We have a ticket to heaven because Jesus paid the cost.
We become His vessels to carry the word to the lost.

We have our ticket to heaven if we accept His love.
He has prepared for us a mansion in heaven above.
While we live in this world, we must witness to men;
Tell the world of Jesus and that He is coming again.

May 19, 2008

Isaiah 4:2; Isaiah 28:5; Isaiah 52:7; Ezekiel 20:6; Acts 3:2; Rev. 22:1-21;
Isaiah 52:11; Isaiah 66:20; Isaiah 29:16; Isaiah 45:9; Isaiah 64:8; Jeremiah 18:4; Zech. 11:13;
Romans 9:21; John 3:14-17; Luke 4:4; Luke 22:19; John 4:10-11;
John 6:7; John 6:31-35; Rev. 7:17

THE TEMPLE

There is a place in heaven where the temple of God stands;
A temple built on a firm foundation, not on sinking sands.
Our heavenly father made it where our Savior reigns.
He wears a crown of gold and a beautiful flowing train.

The ark is in this temple, it contains the budding rod.
The ark contains the word written by the finger of God.
It also contains the manna on which our souls must feed;
To learn the things of the Lord, His words we must read.

I want to go to the place where my Savior doth abide.
He sits on His throne in the temple at His father's side.
He will teach us His words and help us understand.
When He formed the universe, He had us in His plan.

One day we will go to heaven where His love abounds.
We will stand before His holy throne on His holy grounds.
He will teach us many things that to our eyes were dim.
He will give us holy visions that we might look to Him.

The knowledge we have obtained is but a speck of dust.
He wants to give us knowledge to serve Him and to trust.
He has given us many blessings while we live here on earth.
The greatest blessing He ever gave was the gift of new birth.

May 20, 2008

Mark 14:58/ Acts 7:47-50/ Hebrews 9:11-14/ Hebrews 9:21-28/ Zechariah 6:12/ Isaiah 11:1/
Jeremiah 33:15/ Zechariah 3:8/ Zechariah 6:13/ Psalms 72:17-19/ Ephesians 1:17-23/
Revelation 7:15-17/ Revelation 11:19/ Revelation 21:22/
Isaiah 6:1/ Isaiah 66:1

THE RAPTURE

When Jesus comes to take us home, He will come in the by and by.
He will come and take us up so far we will reach that heavenly sky.
When He comes to get His church, the dead in Christ will rise first.
Then those who trust in the Lord will quickly rise from this earth.

Believers will change in an instant with bodies that will not die.
We will go up through the clouds when we meet Him in the sky.
It will be a wonderful reunion when we see our Savior and friend.
We will be with our families in heaven, then eternity will begin.

The Lord will meet us in the air and take us to our home above.
He has prepared the marriage supper, a meal prepared with love.
Saints will receive new bodies without the afflictions of the old.
We will enter our beautiful mansions and walk the streets of gold.

The church is the bride of Christ; He loved us so He gave His life.
He calls us to be with Him and give up this world of sin and strife.
If we look to His word, it tells us by His signs He is coming soon.
Only the Father knows but the word says morning, night or noon.

Many things are happening that through the prophets were foretold.
The God of the universe is still on His throne and He is in control.
Man may think he can change God's word and write a new chapter.
The word of God will never change and the next thing is the rapture.

May 24, 2008

1 Corinthians 15:45-58; 2 Cor. 12:2; 2 Cor. 12:4; 1 Thes. 4:17; Rev. 12:5; Psalm 4:5;
Psalm 31:6; Proverbs 3:5; Genesis 35:2; Psalm 102:26; Matthew 18:3;
Matthew 25:10; Mark 2:19-20; Rev. 18:23; Rev. 22:7; Luke 14:16-26;
1 Cor. 11:20-21; Rev. 19:9; Romans 7:4; Ephes. 5:21-25; Matthew 22:1-14

THE LITTLE BOAT

There was a little boat going up and down the river.
When he blew his whistle, it made a person shiver.
The little boat was proud when he traveled upstream,
But when he blew his whistle, it took a lot of steam.

It took a lot of effort and his boiler was about to pop.
When he blew his whistle, he almost came to a stop.
We are like that boat when we blow our whistle loud.
When we blow our whistle without God, we are proud.

We like to get the credit for all the things we do.
We need to give God credit and to Him be true.
When we work for the Lord He gives us strength.
We need to be faithful and always give him thanks.

We must give credit to God for the things we do.
We must give God the credit and to Him be true.
God will see us through all the storms of life.
God will help us deal with all our daily strife.

December 13, 2008

Luke 19:37; 2 Cor. 9:13; John 9:24; Proverbs 11:2; Eccles. 7:8; Isaiah 25:11; Jeremiah 13:17;
Daniel 5:20; Amos 8:7; Galatians 6:4; James 1:9-10

49

THE IMAGE

Nebuchadnezzar dreamed of an image made of many metals.
This dream was very confusing and it left his mind unsettled.
He called for his wise men to show him what he had dreamed.
Astrologers and magicians could not tell him what he had seen.

They said, "O king, live forever and tell us what you dreamed,
Then we will give the interpretation of what you have seen."
The king then replied, "This dream has gone from my mind,
If you are men of wisdom, the right answers you will find."

They could not give the interpretation so they stalled for time.
If the King would tell them what he dreamed, it would be fine.
They could not answer because they did not know God's will.
The king became very angry and these wise men he would kill.

The Chaldeans said to the King, "How can you ask such a thing?"
The King was very angry so he made a decree that they be slain.
Then Arioch made known to Daniel the things that were going on.
Daniel asked the King for time so he could make the dream known.

Then Daniel and his friends prayed to the God of the universe.
They prayed He would reveal the dream and the decree reverse.
God gave Daniel a night vision and the dream was revealed.
God gave Daniel the interpretation and no one would be killed.

Daniel blessed the Lord God and gave Him honor and praise.
Daniel said, "God creates empires and kingdoms He does raise.
He reveals all the secret things, and brings them to the light.
He is the King of Kings and the word does show His might."

Daniel goes to Arioch and asks for an audience with the King.
He could tell this dream and the interpretation of these things.
The King said to Daniel, "Can you truly tell me this dream?"
Daniel said, "Your wise men could not reveal this to the King."

"Blessed is our God for wisdom and might are in His hands.
To you, O King, He reveals all things according to His plans.
He came to me in a night vision and told me of this dream.
Now, only through the God of creation can I tell it to the King."

"Your dream was of an image, a man most awesome to see.
When you awoke you wondered what this dream could be.
God has given you a vision, O king, of the empires that will be.
When I give the interpretation, you must reverse your decree."

When Daniel spoke to the king God helped him to be bold.
"The metallic image that you saw, O king, had a head of gold."
As Daniel described the image, the king started to shiver.
"The breast and arms of the image were made of pure silver."

"The belly and thighs came next and they were made of brass."
If we saw this image today, we would say the artist had class.
"His legs were of iron and his feet were part iron and part clay."
The image had been described, but Daniel had a lot more to say.

"In this dream, you saw a stone cut out without human hands.
This stone comes from the God above to complete His plans.
This stone struck the image upon his feet of iron and clay.
The image was made into chaff and the wind carried it away."

"The stone became a great mountain and filled the whole earth."
God had destroyed all evil and a new empire was given birth.
The dream had been given but the king had demanded more.
The king wanted the interpretation; he had to know the score.

Daniel said to the king, "God has made you the head of gold.
Power, strength and glory are yours, and a kingdom to behold.
The breast and arms of silver are an empire inferior to thee.
These are the things that my God has allowed the king to see."

51

"A third kingdom shall rule all the earth represented by brass."
With each kingdom Daniel described the value became less.
"The legs of iron were the fourth kingdom that would surely be.
This kingdom would last the longest but then it would cease."

"The fourth kingdom would be revived, represented by the feet."
When the world sees the revived kingdom, they think it is neat.
This kingdom is made of iron and clay, which makes it weak.
The word of God says this kingdom will crumble in a week.

This kingdom will crumble in seven years; each day is a year.
Those who have not put their faith in the stone will live in fear.
The stone will strike the mighty image at the weakest point.
The feet made of iron and clay will break apart at every joint.

"The whole image, from head to toe, will be turned into chaff."
For seven long years, this mighty image will face God's wrath.
"The chaff of the image will be carried away by a mighty wind."
There will be peace on earth and for a thousand years, no sin.

"The stone that comes from the mountain will fill the earth."
The God who created the universe will bring forth new birth.
Jesus, our Lord and Savior, will reign for a thousand years.
If we choose to follow Jesus, He will wipe away all our tears.

January 16, 2009

Daniel 2; 2 Chron. 36:5-7; Jeremiah 25:1-12; Ezra 1:1-10; Leviticus 19:26;
Isaiah 44:25; Proverbs 16:14; Matthew 20:25; Proverbs 3:4-6; Romans 15:30; Psalms 103:1-4;
Deuteronomy 29:29; Psalm 37:30; Psalm 51:6; Proverbs 1:7; Proverbs 1:20; Amos 4:13;
Jeremiah 27:6-7; Jeremiah 5:15; Isaiah 45:1-5;
Daniel 5:28-31; Daniel 7:5; Micah 4:1-5; Isaiah 45:1-5; Psalm 118:22; Isaiah 9:6-7

THE TREE (The Nation)

While "I" Nebuchadnezzar rested in my palace one night,
I had a dream on my bed, which gave me much fright.
Again, I called my wise men to make the dream known,
But when they could not interpret it, it made me groan.

Then Belteshazzar came to me in the name of his God.
When I saw this servant, I bid him come with a nod.
Then I told Belteshazzar about the vision I had seen.
It was very common for him to interpret my dreams.

I told my servant, "I saw a tree in the middle of a field."
When I saw this tree standing there it gave me a chill.
The tree grew very tall and fed all who came there.
They made their homes in the tree and had not a care.

It was filled with leaves, a very pleasant sight to see.
It was filled with much fruit, as plentiful as can be.
All the beasts and birds came from the land around,
But this mighty tree was about to be brought down.

This watcher from Heaven said, "Cut this tree down."
Strip off its leaves and scatter its fruit to the ground.
Let all the beasts and birds be scattered from this tree,
But leave the roots and stump standing up to the knee.

The Man (The King)

The watcher said his heart is changed from a man's.
Give him the heart of a beast for this is God's plan.
The stump will be bound and the grass wet with dew.
He will live in the wild and all this grass he will chew.

Let seven times pass over him by the watcher's decree,
That the most High God rules and His words must be.
This dream I had Belteshazzar, your God can interpret it.
My wise men were not able to make it known by their wit.

Then Daniel was astonished when he spoke to this king,
So I told Daniel, "Be not troubled to interpret this dream."

Daniel said, "May this dream be to them that hate thee."
"And may the interpretation thereof be to all thy enemy."

This tree reached to Heaven and its fruit was quite a treat.
Birds and beast came to the tree and its fruit they did eat.
The leaves were so beautiful they were a great temptation.
Belteshazzar, through his God, gave me the interpretation.

The Interpretation

The tree, O King, is you, for your kingdom has truly grown.
It reaches to the heavens and your dominion is very strong.
This watcher is from Heaven who said cut down this tree.
He comes from the Holy One who has declared this decree.

The grass is wet, the stump and the roots left in the earth.
After seven times passes over you, there will be a new birth.
This is the interpretation: you will be driven from all men.
You will live like a beast and eat the wet grass like oxen.

You will be wet with dew from Heaven until seven times pass.
Belteshazzar was giving me the interpretation just as I had asked.
These things would happen to me until I knew the Most High.
He is ruler in all the kingdoms of men and He cannot tell a lie.

Belteshazzar had tried to warn me of the things that would be,
But my heart would not accept it and my eyes could not see.
He told me to change my ways and break off from my sins.
Show mercy to the poor so my tranquility God would extend.

Fulfilled Prophecy

I was in my palace and twelve months had come and gone.
I was thinking of my power and the majesty of my throne.
I built this kingdom of Babylon for my glory and majesty.
I was the greatest on the earth; what more could a king be?

Then a voice came from heaven and fell sharp upon my ear.
It caused my heart to tremble and my soul it caused to fear.
This voice said to me, "The kingdom is departed from thee."
Your mighty kingdom has been cut down just like the tree.

You shall dwell with beasts of the field and eat the wet grass.
Your kingdom is ruled by gods represented by iron and brass.
That hour I ate with the beasts and my body was wet with dew.
My hair was like eagles' feathers; my nails like birds' claws grew.

When seven times passed by, the number of years was seven.
I lifted up my eyes and gave praise to the Holy One of heaven.
My kingdom was reestablished and greatness was added to me.
The king of heaven took my pride and made me humble, you see.

We gave glory and honor to Him for His kingdom is everlasting.
We must look to the true King for men's kingdoms are passing.
When we turn from the words of God, He puts us in our place.
Those who refuse to follow His commands, He is able to abase.

April 18, 2009

Daniel 4:1-37; Psalms 51:14; Psalms 71:19; Psalms 66:16; Job 7:13-14; Isaiah 44:25; Jeremiah 27:9-10; Daniel 1:19-21; Deut. 29:29; Daniel 1:17; Psalms 37:35-36; Jeremiah 12:1-3; Isaiah 10:33-34; Ezekiel 31:3-18; Mark 4:30-34; Jeremiah 27:6-7; Ezekiel 17:20-24; Daniel 5:20; Mathew 7:19; Luke 3:9; Jeremiah 51:1-10; Mark 5:4-5; Job 12:24; Luke 24:38; Psalm 106:19-21; James 4:6-7; 1 Samuel 2:3; Ezekiel 21:26

FOUR BEASTS

While Belshazzar ruled in Babylon, Daniel had a dream.
Daniel wrote the dream down and told what he had seen.
I saw in my vision one night four winds on the great sea.
Four great beasts came from the sea as diverse as can be.

One was like a lion and with swift eagle wings, it struck.
It was lifted from the earth and its wings were plucked.
This beast was changed and on two feet made to stand.
This beast was changed and given the heart of a man.

The second was like a bear and was raised up on one side.
He devoured the flesh of three ribs when they said arise.
One was like a leopard with four birds wings on its back.
It had four heads and dominion and gave very little slack.

The fourth beast was so terrible it was hard to describe.
It destroyed everything; it seemed nothing would survive.
With great iron teeth, it devoured and tore everything apart.
It seemed this beast wanted to destroy for it had no heart.

He was different from all the rest and he stomped in a rage.
He was like a wild animal which had escaped from his cage.
He was different from those before him for he had ten horns.
When he is through, many will wish that he had not been born.

Three horns were plucked out; a little one took over as king.
It had eyes of a man and a mouth which spoke great things.
Many would follow this beast, which came up as a little horn.
We need to listen to God for by His words He tries to warn.

Then I saw the Ancient of Days; white as snow was His attire.
His hair was like pure wool and His throne had wheels of fire.
Many ministered to Him; from His throne came a fiery stream.
Many thousands stood before Him; books were open to be seen.

Because of the voice of the little horn, he was given to be slain.
The other beasts survived a little while but would lose their fame.
The beast, known as the little horn, was to be destroyed by fire.
He had tried to take God's place and His downfall was his desire.

I saw coming in the clouds of Heaven one as the son of man.
He stood before the Ancient of Days and was given God's plan.
He was given dominion and glory, and a kingdom everlasting.
He will rule over the nations for men's kingdoms are passing.

My spirit grieved my body and these visions troubled me.
I asked the one who stood by what the interpretation could be.
These four beasts are kings who from this earth shall arise.
Saints take the kingdom when the Lord comes from the skies.

Of the fourth beast, with teeth of iron, I had to know the truth.
Why this beast with nails of brass would be turned loose?
He will destroy and break in pieces everything in his path.
Then the Lord of heaven will come and destroy him at last.

These ten horns are kingdoms that this little horn will rule.
He desires to take God's place and for power, he doth drool.
He speaks against the Most High and wears out the saints.
He fools many people with the word pictures that he paints.

He will have a lot of power and change times and the law.
But he will trip himself up by the lies that stick in his craw.
His time is short, it will be time and times and half a time,
Then Christ comes with His saints and all things will be fine.

The judgment is set, and to his kingdom, they make an end.
Christ will come with a trumpet sound for He is our friend.
The kingdom of Christ is the greatest through all eternity.
His desire is to give salvation and for all men to set us free.

April 25, 2009

Daniel 7:1-28; Rev. 13:1; Jeremiah 4:7&13; Jeremiah 25:38; Jeremiah 48:40;
Matthew 24:28; Rev. 13:2; Hosea 13:8

LIFELINE

Jesus is our lifeline and He hears our every call.
He is with us every step and He knows if we should fall.
He watches over us and He is connected to our home.
He keeps in touch with us without using a telephone.

We do not need a button to make a direct connection.
When we fall He helps us make the right correction.
He is always there for us, twenty-four and seven.
He will meet our needs from His throne in heaven.

When we are in trouble, He hears our every plea.
He comes to our rescue and our troubles do flee.
He is our personal contact to God's salvation plan.
The contact is free for at Golgotha He took a stand.

We can do His will when we care for one another.
We can show His love when we care for our brother.
We can show His love when we tell of His grace,
When He died upon the cross and took our place.

April 30, 2009

2 Samuel 23:5; Psalm 18:2; Psalm 67:2; Psalm 118:21; Micah 7:7; John 19:17;
Luke 10:34-35; Ex. 15:2; Rom. 11:11; 1 Cor. 10:12; 2 Pet. 1:10; 1 Cor. 1:25;
1 Pet. 5:7

THE LION'S DEN

Daniel was governor when Darius was the king.
Daniel prayed to God above but not to be seen.
The others were jealous and lies they would tell.
He did what was right and served Darius well.

To get rid of Daniel the other governors sought.
Daniel was faithful to follow what God taught.
He respected the king and did what was right.
He prayed to God and was blessed by His might.

When they found no fault in Daniel's character,
They devised a clever scam using another factor.
They appealed to the king knowing of his pride.
They needed to get the king to come to their side.

They talked the king into making a firm decree.
They knew when he heard this he would agree.
Everyone was commanded to pray to the king.
When Darius heard this he thought it a fine thing.

Darius signed the decree making this thing a law.
He did not know this decree had a terrible flaw.
He had no intention of putting Daniel in a bind.
Daniel was his friend and to the king he was kind.

When Daniel heard this, he went to God to pray.
He knelt in his room as he did three times a day.
He faced Jerusalem with his windows open wide.
His enemy was listening to him from just outside.

Going to the king, with this news, they were quick.
The scam was working and their plan did the trick.
When Darius heard the news, his heart began to sink.
He had to free his friend, he needed time to think.

The men told the king, "The decree you have signed.
Daniel broke the law and must be cast to the lions.
Your word is the law, O king, this thing must be done."
At this point the king's men were having a lot of fun.

The king felt very sorrowful he had signed the decree.
He wanted very much to find a way to set Daniel free.
The king could think of nothing, the die had been cast.
It seemed that poor Daniel would soon breathe his last.

Daniel was cast into the den, the king placed his seal.
The king went to his palace but refused to eat a meal.
No musical instrument played in the palace that night.
The king slept not a wink but was about at first light.

When he came to the den he cried out to his friend.
Had Daniel survived or had his life come to an end?
He asked, "O Daniel, has your God seen you through?
Is this mighty God you serve the one that is true?"

Then Daniel cried to the king, "O king live forever.
My God has sent His angel and He is able to deliver.
He shut the lions' mouths and they brought no harm.
He found me innocent and there is no need for alarm."

Then Darius commanded that the stone be rolled away.
Daniel came from the lions den with no harm that day.
Those who accused Daniel were thrown into the den.
When we go against God there is no way we can win.

Then the king made a decree that all should serve God.
His kingdom will be forever and He rules with His rod.
When Jesus, His Son, comes to rule, every knee will bow.
All the wars will cease and the sword made into a plow.

ABRAHAM

God promised Abram that he would have a son,
And his descendants would become a great nation.
That this nation would prosper and it would grow.
This would be God's nation with blessings to bestow.

Abram left his family wandering for many years.
He would go at God's command facing many fears.
With his wife Sarai he wondered through the land.
He trusted in God and followed His guiding hand.

He came to a land that to this nation would belong.
God had brought him there for He can do no wrong.
God had shown him land but the time had not come.
The years had passed by, but still there was not a son.

He came with his nephew Lot, they divided the land.
Lot chose to go to Sodom, but God had another plan.
God would destroy Sodom by fire for her sinful way.
It had become wicked and God would have His say.

Sarai had no child so she gave Abram her handmaid.
Far beyond child bearing she thought God had delayed.
She went beyond the will of God and did things her way.
She should have trusted God, for His will we must obey.

Abram went in to Hagar and she bore him a son.
Taking Sarai's advice, he knew what he had done.
Hagar's son would be the beginning of many nations,
But it was God's will that Sarai would have a son.

Abram would not have peace while Hagar stayed.
Discord would arise between Sarai and her maid.
Sarai became angry and in her soul she did relent.
Sarai wanted Abram to send Hagar from his tent.

Hagar fled from Sarai and to a fountain she came.
An angel appeared to Hagar giving her son his name.
The angel said to Hagar, "To your mistress return.
Call your son, Ishmael, from his father he must learn."

Hagar bore this son but he would become a wild man.
Every man was against him, he would have no friend.
He would father many nations, but he was God's enemy.
They would be blessed by God but they rebelled, you see.

The Lord came to Abram, he was ninety-nine years old.
He was reminded of God's covenant just as he was told.
God said to Abram, "Be thou perfect and walk with me.
I will keep my covenant and exceedingly multiply thee."

God said to Abram, "Your seed I will surely multiply.
You must keep My covenant and circumcision not deny.
You shall father many and Abraham will be your name.
You must honor Me and your descendants do the same.

Sarai will be called Sarah and she shall give you a son.
Sarah shall become the mother of My anointed nation.
My everlasting covenant will be with him and his seed.
His descendants must honor Me and I will meet their need."

God's messengers told Abraham of these things to come.
Then they reminded Abraham that he was to have a son.
Sarah heard what the Lord said and laughed out loud.
She should have listened carefully and been very proud.

The men turned their faces and went toward Sodom.
Surely the souls of that wicked city had hit rock bottom.
Abraham made his plea for in his soul he had great pity.
How many righteous souls would it take to save the city?

Fifty, forty, thirty or twenty or could even ten be found?
Alas, this city of Sodom was built on unstable ground.
Because Abraham had prayed, Lot's family would survive.
The messengers sent by God would snatch them out alive.

When Lot saw the Angels coming he rose to meet them.
He could not leave them in the street or even at an inn.
He took them to his home and gave them personal care.
They could not be caught up in the city's wicked snare.

When they heard what Lot did they came to his house.
Lot refused to give up the men so they started a rouse.
Lot would give his daughters to God's men, he was kind.
These men of God had power to strike the people blind.

The men said to Lot, "Take your family from this place.
God said to destroy Sodom for this is a very wicked race."
Lot was reluctant, but the Angels sent them on their way.
Sodom was so sinful that God would have the final say.

Lot's family left Sodom with their provisions in a sack.
Lot's wife disobeyed God when she turned to look back.
She loved the worldly Sodom and she could find no fault.
But when she looked back she turned into a pillar of salt.

Abraham looked to Sodom and saw smoke as a furnace.
When God has spoken His words, He does it in earnest.
God destroyed other cities, one was called Gomorrah.
God spared a little city for Lot wanted to go to Zoar.

Lot lived in a cave where he committed fornication.
His daughters bore sons which began wicked nations.
From that time till this day they became God's enemy.
God's children and these nations would have rivalry.

The Lord visited Sarah, and as He promised, she conceived.
Abraham and Sarah should have trusted God and believed.
This was the son God promised and Isaac was his name.
Sarah heard the Lord's words and from her laughter came.

This son was circumcised according to God's command.
As the child grew, Sarah came to Abraham with her demand.
Sarah said to Abraham, "This son, Ishmael, is not your heir.
You must give to your promised son Isaac all your care."

God said to Abraham, "Let it not be grievous in thy sight.
He is thy seed and of him shall grow a nation by My might.
You must hearken to the will of Sarah and hear her voice,
For Isaac is the promised son and I have made My choice."

Abraham gave Hagar and Ishmael water and sent them away.
The water ran out so they set down and Hagar began to pray.
God heard the voice of the lad and sent an angel to their aid.
The angel showed them a well of water and said be not afraid.

God had spared Ishmael because he was Abraham's son.
Isaac and his descendants became God's chosen nation.
Ishmael was a nomad and in the wilderness he did roam.
The descendants of Isaac would make Canaan their home.

As time passed by and Isaac grew, God did test Abraham.
He told Abraham to make a sacrifice but not to use a lamb.
Take thy son and offer him up on the place I will show thee.
Go to Moriah and make an offering of thy son and obey me.

Abraham made preparation and laid wood on Isaac's back.
Preparations were taken care of but a lamb they did lack.
It had taken three days and Abraham would sacrifice his son.
Of all the tests Abraham had this was the hardest he had done.

Isaac asked, "Where is the lamb? We have fire and wood."
Abraham said, "God provides a lamb for only He could."
Then Abraham bound his son and placed him on the altar.
When Abraham took the knife in his hand would he falter?

An angel of God said, "Lay not thy hand upon the lad."
By doing what God has said, you have made Him glad.
Because you fear the Lord a sacrifice He will provide.
By faith you trusted God and your needs are not denied."

Then Abraham saw the ram where before there was none.
This ram had become the burnt offering instead of his son.
Abraham called the place, Jehovah-jireh, for God did provide.
When we obey the Lord's will our needs will not be denied.

August 2009

65

THE TEN VIRGINS

There were ten virgins in their chamber on that day,
As they waited for the groom to take the bride away.
They knew He would come but they knew not when.
His coming was sure and on that they could depend.

Their lamps had been filled and trimmed with care,
But five were foolish for they had no oil to spare.
The other five were wise, they had plenty to spare.
The oil was for their lamps, they could not share.

As they set in their chamber waiting for the groom,
The oil in their lamps would be gone very soon.
When their oil got low the foolish began to fret.
They would have to leave for precious oil to get.

They left the chamber hoping for some oil to find.
Maybe they would see someone who would be kind.
The others stayed in the chamber, they were prepared.
They knew the groom would come and not be deterred.

When the groom came knocking at the door that night,
The wise virgins were ready for they had plenty of light.
The five that were wise were those that were received.
The wise were prepared but the foolish were deceived.

Have you prepared your lamp for the groom's return?
Is your lamp filled with oil which you cannot earn?
The oil that you must have the Lord will provide.
This oil is free for everyone but you must decide.

Come to Christ and He will give you His Precious oil.
Do not be like other souls and for worldly things toil.

February 6, 2010

SERVANTS

Thank God for public servants who take care of us,
Even when we rant and rave and start up such a fuss.
They do their very best to keep this nation on the go,
But they get very little praise or our thanks to bestow.

They are out in the bad weather to keep our power on,
As their families wait and pray they return safely home.
Their job takes them out on cold and stormy nights,
Just to give our homes plenty of comfort and lights.

They face many dangers as they repair the power line.
We should realize that to make these repairs takes time.
We become impatient as the minutes tick slowly by,
But with these servants on the job we can surely rely.

With the lightning flashing and the wind blowing strong,
Let us pray for their safety that nothing would go wrong.
Let us give them the respect that they so justly deserve.
They are always on the job and they are ready to serve.

February 18, 2010

NURSES

Let us thank God for nurses who give us loving care.
They come to our bedside with healing hands to share.
They come with loving hearts and meet all our needs.
Thank God for their kindness while on bended knees.

As servants of those who are sick they truly passed the test.
With their skills they serve us, sometimes with little rest.
They are there at our bedside like angels from above,
With healing hands of mercy and hearts filled with love.

The Doctors have their knowledge in healing, that is true,
But without nurses by their side there is little they can do.
They help comfort our bodies and give us peace of mind.
Even when we complain they try their best to be kind.

I've never seen an ugly nurse, they have beauty we can see.
They are the patient ones when they take care of you and me.
I know that they grow weary as they serve their fellow man,
But as they go about their tasks they are a part of God's plan.

Their tasks may differ from the aid to the registered nurse,
But their goal remains the same for they all take care of us.
Sometimes we fail to thank them as they give their life to serve.
We need to give them our love and the gratitude they deserve.

March 16, 2010

FAMILY FARMER

Thank God for family farmers who grow our food today.
They serve our country in the good old American way.
They work from dawn till dusk and sometimes in the night.
But to keep these farms going they really have to fight.

When they make a bumper crop the price goes down.
When bad years comes, some say, "Let the farmer drown."
These families have to work very hard to live and survive.
But even when on the bottom they keep this country alive.

The family farmer believes that God and country come first.
While some others believe they should worship mother earth.
Many of those who started America were tillers of the land.
When they signed the Constitution they had soil in their hand.

Knowing working people would keep this nation on the go.
They passed laws to protect them and help this nation grow.
These laws they passed have been changed through the years.
They've been added to and taken from causing many tears.

We need to get back to our roots and back to fertile ground.
We need to till the soil of truth and faith and let freedom sound.
Some people think freedom is doing anything you want to.
True freedom is being responsible for all the things you do.

April 22, 2010

CARPENTER

Carpenters are a special breed working with wood.
If they could build a perfect heart I know they would.
It would be built from the choicest wood they could find.
They would shape it with much care and make it kind.

They would take the best tree in the forest all around.
This wood would last forever and make a joyful sound.
This heart would be in perfect rhythm with its maker.
The carpenter, himself, would be the heart's caretaker.

It would function well and its beat would be strong.
It would be made in a way that nothing would go wrong.
When placed in our body this heart would function well.
Giving us new life, of this carpenter we would want to tell.

We understand that new life a wooden heart cannot give.
Jesus can give us a heart of flesh so eternal life we can live.
Jesus was a carpenter and He is God's only begotten son.
He can give us this new heart and put the devil on the run.

Jesus is the master carpenter who can care for our heart,
If we come to Him and repent He will give us a new start.
This heart we have filled with sin cannot last for eternity.
This new heart that Jesus gives, from sin will set us free.

May 10, 2010

COME, JESUS

Satan will have his last chance for seven years to rule.
Satan's desire is to rule all the earth and sin is his tool.
Before Satan takes over all believers will be caught up.
This earth will begin to shake and disasters will erupt.

Men become fearful as their world begins to falls apart.
They think by the things they do we will have a new start.
They must look to Jesus who was sent by the God of love.
We must look to our Jesus for our strength is from above.

Brethren, be not discouraged for Jesus is coming again.
He will fight the greatest battle and He will surely win.
The saints will hear the Archangel and the trumpet call.
Lord Jesus will take His rightful place and rule over all.

Jesus, the faithful witness, knows the history of this earth.
Jesus, the firstborn, gave His life to give us a new birth.
Jesus, the Prince of Kings, to Him every knee will bow.
Jesus Christ, who loves us, gives us a new heart if we allow.

Jesus gave His precious blood which washed away our sin.
Jesus makes us priests and kings and if we obey Him, we win.
To Him we give glory and dominion down through the ages.
You learn these things about our Lord in Revelation pages.

July 9, 2010

GIVE PRAISE

O Lord, I will exalt thee, for you have lifted me up.
O Lord, you have blessed me and filled my cup.
O Lord, you have brought my soul from the grave.
When I was lost in sin, for you died my soul to save.

I sing unto the Lord and to Him my thanks I give.
Because of His wonderful love I have learned to live.
As my enemies come against me there is a forlorning.
Weeping comes in the night but joy comes in morning.

O Lord, you have made my mountain to stand strong.
I put my faith in you, Lord, for you can do no wrong.
No profit is in my blood but your blood saves from sin.
You gave your blood at Calvary that in victory I win.

Even when I slip and fall, Lord you stay by my side.
You have given me the Holy Spirit to be my guide.
I am in Your hands, Lord, and You will not let me go.
You give me grace and mercy and blessings bestow.

July 25, 2010

PERFECT LOVE

Jesus came to this world to show His perfect love.
He came from God in heaven from His throne above.
He came to teach God's word and show men the way.
He came to shape men's lives and mold them like clay.

He made them into vessels to carry the word of God.
He came to free men so they might go where He trod.
He gave them His holy light to show them the way,
Along this trail of darkness where man goes astray.

He gives the bread of life to feed the souls of men,
That their spirit be fed that they never hunger again.
He gave us eternal life by giving His life on the cross.
Then He sent us into the world to witness to the lost.

August 4, 2010

EIGHT PENNIES

Eight little pennies are all they had to give.
They gave all they had so others might live.
Eight pennies to help a mother, child or wife,
Of Wounded warrior soldiers who give their life.

Eight pennies can do more than you know.
When they become seeds that sprout and grow.
It is so little, yet it is so much for those who die.
Hearing of what they gave should make us cry.

You might criticize when you hear such a thing.
The widow's mites caused heaven's bells to ring.
Just give what you can and may GOD bless it all.
Pray for our soldiers as they defend freedom's call.

August 16, 2010

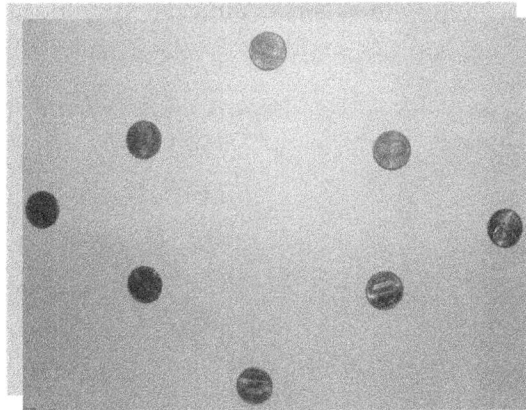

MY LOOK ALIKE

Athens, my great nephew, is as cute as he can be.
When he was born, they said he looked a lot like me.
I would not dispute their word for he is a fine lad.
But when I show our picture some think I am mad.

When I was his age, everyone thought I was cute,
However, as I get older, the more I get the boot.
I felt very good when they said he looked like me,
Then someone said they might need glasses to see.

Now I have cataracts and my sight is growing dim.
When my sight returns I think I will still look like him.
Even if we do not resemble I will be proud to know,
That to the skeptics I have this picture I can show.

In this life, there is little that gives us real pleasure.
But when it comes to my look alike, he is a treasure.
I hope that when he grows up into a fine young man,
He'll show this picture and say, "I am from this Clan."

October 14, 2010

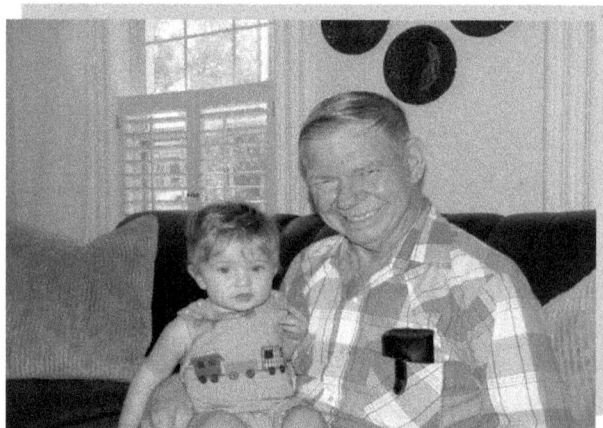

NABOTH'S VINEYARD

Ahab, the king of Israel, did evil in the sight of the Lord.
When he could not have his way, he became quite bored.
He wanted Naboth's vineyard but could not get his way.
Then Jezebel, the queen, said she would have the final say.

She would devise a plan to have Naboth falsely accused.
To get what the king wanted no plan would be excused.
She hired false witnesses and for money they would lie.
She told Ahab to cheer up for there was no need to cry.

To accuse Naboth of blasphemy their lies they would tell.
But Jezebel was wrong for she served the idol called Baal.
By her evil and false accusations, she had Naboth stoned.
Ahab would get the vineyard while Naboth was wronged.

It seems that sometimes in this world that evil will prevail.
But God's judgment would come upon Ahab and Jezebel.
God called upon Elijah to speak to the wicked king, Ahab.
God's judgment would surely come and there was no rehab.

Elijah said to Ahab, "You have done evil in God's sight.
Because of this thing He will cut you off by His might.
I will bring calamity on you and cut you off from men.
You caused me anger for against me you committed sin."

"Your house will become like Jeroboam, the son of Nebat.
The evil you committed against Naboth you will regret.
Then dogs will eat the flesh of the wicked queen, Jezebel.
She has committed abomination by serving the idol Baal."

When Ahab heard this judgment, in sackcloth he did lay.
Then God spoke to Elijah, "My judgment I will delay."
Ahab remained the same while three years had passed by.
There was no justice while the blood of Naboth did cry.

But, when it comes to the word of God He is not slack.
When God declares that vengeance is His, He must act.
The king of Judah came to Ahab asking to make a pact.
They would make an alliance and Syria they would attack.

Jehoshaphat asks if a prophet of the Lord could be found.
He needed to know that they were acting on solid ground.
But, Ahab trusted his prophets and on them he would call.
The false Prophets said go, for the Syrians shall surely fall.

Jehoshaphat insisted that a prophet of the Lord be found.
Then Ahab said to Jehoshaphat, Micaiah might be around.
Then Ahab said this prophet does not speak well of his king.
Then Jehoshaphat replied, "Do not speak of such a thing."

They called for the prophet Micaiah but told him what to say.
Micaiah agreed to see the king but would do so in God's way.
Ahab's prophets made horns of iron and put on quite a show.
But Micaiah was a man of God and the truth he would know.

The messenger asked Micaiah to speak words that were kind.
Micaiah told the king to fight and everything would be fine.
The king became angry and said, "The truth you must tell.
Never when speaking of me have you said all would be well."

Then Micaiah told King Ahab this battle would be at a cost.
Like stray sheep without a shepherd, many would be lost.
God had sent a lying spirit into the false prophets of Baal.
These spirits deceived the king by saying all would go well.

Then King Ahab had Micaiah locked away in a prison cell.
By God's hands, justice would come to Ahab and Jezebel.
Ahab would go into battle and the Syrians he would fight.
All the Syrian soldiers wanted to get Ahab in their sight.

Ahab had disguised himself and thought that he was safe,
But you cannot hide from the Lord and this was the case.
There was a man who drew his bow and let his arrow fly.
He knew not where the arrow went but Ahab was to die.

The king was hit in a vital place and blood began to flow.
He told his driver he was wounded and from the battle go.
The king was taken to Samaria and buried, for he had died.
The chariot was washed and dogs licked blood as it dried.

Many years came and went and Jezebel was still around.
Elijah told of her death for blood cried from the ground.
When Jehu became king, old Jezebel had to take a look.
When the king looked at her painted face that is all it took.

Jezebel was thrown from her window high above the street.
Her body hit the ground with a thud and became dog meat.
Jehu's chariot ran over her and he left her body in the street.
When told to bury her they found her skull, hands and feet.

God's justice was fulfilled and Queen Jezebel was no more.
What God has spoken it must be done for that is the score.
Did Ahab truly repent or was he just sorry he was caught.
We need Jesus Christ for by Him our salvation is bought.

January 26, 2011

THE TRUE SHEPHERD

The Lord speaks unto His prophet Ezekiel concerning the last days.
Prophesy to the shepherds that they not treat the flock in these ways.
Woes to you, O wicked shepherds, for you are not feeding my sheep.
You take for yourself the very best and trample the rest under feet.

The flock is scattered through the mountains and every high hill.
There they wander and become food for all the beasts of the field.
You do not seek those who are lost or take care of those who are ill.
They become weak in their wandering and left for the beast to kill.

Therefore, shepherds, hear My voice; listen carefully to what I say.
I am against the shepherds because my flock has become their prey.
You will not feed my flock anymore, so for My sheep I will seek.
I will search and seek them out, for their souls I will take to keep.

I will bring them out of nations and bring them into their land.
I will feed and care for them because they are a part of my plan.
I will feed them in good pastures, in valleys and on mountaintops.
I will give them fertile lands and they will grow abundant crops.

I will bind up the broken and sick, the weak I will make strong.
I will judge those of my flock and destroy those who did wrong.
I will judge those who push and shove as they look into My face.
The righteous among My flock I will surely judge by My grace.

I will make David their prince and will make a covenant of peace.
They will dwell safely in the land and cause the wild beast to cease.
The trees of the field shall yield their fruit, the earth's its increase.
They shall dwell in the land; and from burdens I give them release.

I will make them a garden, no longer will hunger in the land be.
They shall not be prey for the nations for they shall dwell safely.
They are flocks of my pasture, I am their God, and they know me.
My shepherd will soon take His place, follow Him and be set free.

February 24, 2011

Ezekiel 34

ON THE FARM

When we grew up on the farm, we were early from sleep to arouse.
After dad had kindled the fire, he went to feed and milk the cows.
There was much for mother to do getting us kids ready for school.
Her biscuits, grits, eggs and ham always made our taste buds drool.

When we grew up on the farm, life was simple, but things were good.
We had chores to do, like gathering eggs and bringing in the firewood.
We had games to play out in the yard under that great big oak tree.
None of these electronic games in our rooms just punching a key.

We played marbles, leapfrog, hopscotch and other games so neat.
To get to see the cowboy movies on Saturday was a special treat.
We would roll our hoop with a stick and roll down a hill in a tire.
We would walk the pig paths in the woods with our feet in the mire.

We had homemade toys like whistles made from hollow reeds.
Like Tarzan, we would swing from long vines hanging in trees.
We did not spend hundreds of dollars for games to play inside.
We got out in the world of God's creation to get our exercise.

There were horses to ride, trees to climb, and lots of fun to be had.
When we did not get what we wanted, there was no time to get mad.
We learned at a very early age that our parents we had better obey.
It was not uncommon for children to get a spanking in that day.

Our parents were very good to us and provided what we needed,
But they often said no to things not good, even though we pleaded.
When we did not get things our way there was no need to holler.
When we put up a fuss, we knew that punishment was to follow.

The family sat at the dining table when mealtime came around,
And when the blessing was being said, there was no other sound.
Yes, we had it good on the farm and there were hard times too.
We just thanked the Lord for good times and all He would do.

July 13, 2011

THE GOOD OLD DAYS

They were the best of times and the worst of times. Maybe that is the way it has always been, depending on the circumstances of your life. For me, growing up in the 40s and 50s was the best of life, but for many it was not so good. I was born January 9, 1943, and the United States was in the middle of World War 2, but I knew little of that. All I knew was the love of my mother and father and their care for me. We lived in a house on a hill about two hundred feet off Highway 117 for a short time. It must have been a cold winter because mother said when she threw the dishwater out the kitchen door it froze before it hit the ground. We had not lived there very long when we moved to the farm where I grew up and had plenty of fun things to do.

The great oak tree in the front yard provided most of the play area until I was older. That tree must have been there when Columbus sailed the ocean blue. Some oaks of that type live to be four or five hundred years old and some are even older. Not too many people today can say they played under a tree that was around in Columbus's time. Daddy took a cable and attached it to a limb in the old tree. It had a tire on the end for a swing. It was like a giant pendulum and we could swing back and forth forty or fifty feet with the help of his strong arms.

It was under that oak tree that we played many games. This kept us out of mother's way so she could do her housework. Hopscotch was the girls' favorite, although the boys also liked to play. You play hopscotch by drawing squares on the ground and using a pebble and fancy footwork. You can play marbles in a verity of ways. Boys usually played these games, but some girls were also good players.

One of my favorite games was "Chase the Rabbit." If you have never heard of this, it does not surprise me. I made this game up myself. A little boy and his faithful companion play the game. The companion is any dog that wants to follow the boy. The father also gets involved in the game, but unknowingly. When daddy would till or break the sod with his B John Deere and turning disk, he would start at the outer edge and break toward the middle of the field. When he was almost through, it was time for my part of the game. My companion and I would tread across the plowed ground to the edge of the unbroken area and walk along the edge looking for movement in the grass. When Mr. Rabbit would jump out of the grass to get away from the putt, putt sound of the John Deere tractor, off we would go, my companion on the heels of the rabbit, and me on the heels of my companion. Sometimes we would catch the rabbit and sometimes we would not. When we did catch him, we would take him to the edge of the woods or field and set him free.

I hope that these words have helped you recapture some of your experiences of your childhood. We cannot live in the past but maybe it can help us build a better world.

FROM NOAH TO JESUS

He called his name Noah, saying, this same shall comfort us concerning our work and the toil of our hands, because of the ground, which the Lord hath cursed. Moreover, they that are left of you shall pine away in their iniquity in your enemies' lands; and in the iniquities of their fathers shall they pine away with them. If they shall confess their iniquity, and the iniquity of their fathers, with their trespass which they trespassed against me, and that also they have walked contrary unto me; And that I also have walked contrary unto them, and have brought them into the land of their enemies; if then their uncircumcised hearts be humbled, and they accept the punishment of their iniquity: Then will I remember my covenant with Jacob, and also my covenant with Isaac, and also my covenant with Abraham will I remember; and I will remember the land. And it shall come to pass, when all these things are come upon thee, the blessing and the curse, which I have set before thee, and you shall call them to mind among all the nations, whither the Lord thy God hath driven thee, And shall return unto the Lord thy God, and shall obey his voice according to all that I command thee this day, thou and thy children, with all thy heart, and with all thy soul; Then the Lord thy God will turn thy captivity, and have compassion upon thee, and will return and gather thee from all the nations, whither the Lord thy God hath scattered thee. If any of thy people be driven out unto the outmost parts of heaven, from there will the Lord thy God gather thee, and from there will he fetch thee: And the Lord thy God will bring thee into the land which thy fathers possessed, and thou shall possess it; and he will do thee good, and multiply thee above thy fathers. To fulfill the word of the Lord by the mouth of Jeremiah, until the land had enjoyed her Sabbaths: for as long as she lay desolate she kept Sabbath, to fulfill threescore and ten years. You shall arise, and have mercy upon Zion: for the time to favor her, yea, the set time, is come. For thy servants take pleasure in her stones, and favor the dust thereof. Therefore, the heathen shall fear the name of the Lord and all the kings of the earth thy glory. When the Lord shall build up Zion, he shall appear in his glory. He will regard the prayer of the destitute, and not despise their prayer. Moreover, this whole land shall be desolation, and astonishment; and these nations shall serve the king of Babylon seventy years. And it shall come to pass, when seventy years are accomplished, that I will punish the king of Babylon, and that nation, says the Lord, for their iniquity, and the land of the Chaldeans, and will make it a perpetual desolation. For thus says the Lord, that after seventy years be accomplished at Babylon I will visit you, and perform my good word toward you, in causing you to return to this place. Then shall ye call upon me, and ye shall go and pray unto me, and I will hearken unto you. In addition, ye shall seek me, and find me, when ye shall search for me with all your heart. And I will be found of you, says the Lord: and I will turn away your captivity, and I will gather you from all the nations, and from all the places whither I have driven you, says the Lord; and I will bring you again into the place whence I caused you to be carried away captive. Thus says the Lord; Behold, I will bring again the captivity of Jacob's tents, and have mercy on his dwelling places; and the city shall be built upon her own heap, and the palace shall remain after the manner thereof. I will build thee again, and thou shall be built, O virgin of Israel: thou shall again be adorned with thy tabrets, and shall go forth in the dances of them that make merry. For the Lord hath redeemed Jacob, and ransomed him from the hand of him that was stronger than he was. Therefore they shall come and sing in the height of Zion, and shall flow together to the goodness of the Lord, for wheat, and for wine, and for oil, and for the young of the flock and of the herd: and their soul shall be as a watered garden; and they shall not sorrow any more at all. It shall come to pass, that like as I have watched over them, to pluck up, and to break down, and to throw down, and to destroy, and to afflict; so will I watch over them, to build, and to plant, says the Lord. Behold, the days come, says the Lord, that I will make a new covenant with the house of Israel, and with the house of Judah: Therefore say unto the house of Israel, Thus says the Lord God; I do not this for your sakes, O house of Israel, but for mine holy name's sake, which ye have profaned among the heathen, whither ye went. And I will sanctify my great name, which was profaned among the heathen, which ye have profaned in the midst of them; and the heathen shall know that I am the Lord, says the Lord God, when I shall be sanctified in you before their eyes. For verily I say unto you, That many prophets and righteous men have desired to see those things which ye see, and have not seen them; and to hear those things which ye hear, and have not heard them. Peter came to him, and said, Lord, how oft shall my brother sin against me, and I forgive him. Till seven times? Jesus says unto him, I say not unto thee, seven times: but, until seventy times seven. If ye love me keep my commandments. Humble yourselves in the sight of the Lord and he shall lift you up.

April 15, 2014

REBIRTH OF ISRAEL

Genesis 5:3 And Adam lived 130 years, and begat a son in his own likeness, after his image; and called his name Seth: 130

Genesis 5:6 And Seth lived 105 years, and begat Enos: 105

Genesis 5:9 And Enos lived 90 years, and begat Cainan: 90

Genesis 5:12 And Cainan lived 70 years, and begat Mahalaleel: 70

Genesis 5:15 And Mahalaleel lived 65 years, and begat Jared: 65

Gen. 5:18 And Jared lived an hundred 162 years, and he begat Enoch: 162

Gen. 5:21 And Enoch lived 65 years, and begat Methuselah: 65

Genesis 5:25 And Methuselah lived 187 years, and begat Lamech: 187

Genesis 5:28 And Lamech 182 years, and begat a son: 182
        Genesis 5:29 And he called his name Noah, saying,
This same shall comfort us concerning our work and toil of our hands, because of the ground which the Lord hath cursed.

Genesis 5:32 And Noah was 500 years old: and Noah begat
Shem, Ham, and Japheth.   500

TOTAL YEARS   1,556

Genesis 11:10 These are the generations of Shem:
Shem was 100 years old, and begat Arphaxad 2 years after the flood:
2 years must be added for the flood.   102

Genesis 11:12 And Arphaxad lived 35 years, and begat Salah: 35

Genesis 11:14 And Salah lived 30 years, and begat Eber: 30

Genesis 11:16 And Eber lived 34 years, and begat Peleg: 34

Genesis 11:18 And Peleg lived 30 years, and begat Reu: 30

Genesis 11:20 And Reu lived 32 years, and begat Serug: 32

Genesis 11:22 And Serug lived 30 years, and begat Nahor: 30

Genesis 11:24 And Nahor lived 29 years, and begat Terah: 29

Gen. 11:26 And Terah lived 70, and begat Abram, Nahor, and Haran.   70

                                           TOTAL YEARS   392

  1556
+ 392
 1948 The year Israel was reborn.

Adapted from a book by Perry Stone

Genesis 5:5 And all the days that Adam lived were 930 years: and he died.

Genesis 5:8 And all the days of Seth were 912 years: and he died.

Genesis 5:11 And all the days of Enos were 905 years : and he died.

Genesis 5:14 And all the days of Cainan were 910 years: and he died.

Genesis 5:17 And all the days of Mahalaleel were 895 years: and he died.

Genesis 5:20 And all the days of Jared were 962 years: and he died.

Genesis 5:23-24 And all the days of Enoch were 365 years:
And Enoch walked with God: and he was not; for God took him.

Genesis 5:27 And all the days of Methuselah were 969 years: and he died.

Genesis 5:31 And all the days of Lamech were 777 years: and he died.

Total 7625

I've been asked, "Are the years in the Old Testament the same as they are now?" The answer is yes and no. When men first started calculating time the moon and stars were their timepiece. The new moon started and ended each month. The stars and planets were used to calculate the years. I don't want to get into an in-depth discussion of time calculation because that is not my purpose here. If we believe that the Bible is the inspired word of God then we have to accept it literally, which I do. In the verses listed above they give the age of each man when he died. All but two of these men lived to be around 900 years and above. The youngest of these men to die was Lamech who was 777 years old. This is interesting because the number seven is used many times in scripture to indicate completeness or the end of something. Enoch was 365 years old but never died because he was translated or raptured to Heaven without death. This is interesting also in view of the fact that our year is 365 days. In this list from Adam to Lamech it gives the actual age of the men when they died. When you go to Chapter 11 and start with his son Noah it does not do this. At this point you are probably asking, "What's the point of all this?" At this time I was asking myself the same question.

I had added the ages of these men and got 7625 years, but where would I go from there? Going back to the study of calendars I found that you have to add 3760 years to our present day calendar to get the Hebrew year but what year would I add it to. Something in my spirit told me it had to be a year important to Israel. What would be more important than the year they were reborn (1948)? When I did this I came up with 5708 which had no meaning for me but the same spirit told me to subtract 5708 from the total of the ages of the men in the list above when they died (7625). Which Gave me a very important year (1917). WOW! That took us to WW1 but what happened that year that was significant to Israel. For the answer I went back to the world book.

1948   Rebirth of Israel.
<u>3760</u>   Years added to give Hebrew calendar year.
5708   To be subtracted from total age of men on list.
7625 - 5708 = 1917

March 1917 British took Baghdad after they had lost there on 4/29/1916
Dec. 1917 Gen. Edmund Allenby's forces took Jerusalem.
April 6, 1917 United States declared war on Germany.
In 1917 the Balfour Declaration was signed by James Balfour making the Promise Land a home land for the Jews.
During WW1 Chaim Weizmann improved the method of making acetone and butyl alcohol for explosives used to help win the war. When asked what he wanted for his contribution he replied, "A homeland for the Jews."

2014

THE LIGHT

Sunrise on the mountain is a beautiful sight to see.
Sunrise on the mountain is there for you and me.
When the sunrise comes, it means a new day's start.
Resting in the night, for His work we are set apart.

The beauty of the stars shine as bright as can be.
If not for the darkness no beauty could men see.
The darkness is put there so the light can be seen.
Then the shining stars can send out their beam.

(We need to see the light that comes from above.)
(We need to accept the light that is given in love.)

Though the stars are far away, we see their glow.
The darker the night, the more the light will show.
The light shines so brightly in this world today,
But men see the darkness for they do not pray.

I saw this lamp shining in a window far away.
That lamp was lit by Jehovah to show me the way.
It was put there by a friend who knew I was lost.
That friend gave His life on an old rugged cross.

(We need to see the light that comes from above.)
(We need to accept the light that is given in love.)

The word is the light turning men from their sin.
The word is the truth changing hearts from within.
God's word is His only son who came to give light,
Leading them from darkness so men can live right.

God made the moon and stars to shine in the night.
They help us navigate when we travel by their light.
The moon and planets reflect the light from the sun.
As Christians, we reflect light from God's only son.

(We need to see the light that comes from above.)
(We need to accept the light that is given in love.)